MW01531257

Beware of Talking Snakes:

RELIGION'S FAILURE TO ACHIEVE WORLD PEACE

Beware of
Talking Snakes:

RELIGION'S FAILURE TO
ACHIEVE WORLD PEACE

CARLTON W. LAIRD

Ivy House Publishing Group

www.ivyhousebooks.com

PUBLISHED BY IVY HOUSE PUBLISHING GROUP
5122 Bur Oak Circle, Raleigh, NC 27612
United States of America
919-782-0281
www.ivyhousebooks.com

ISBN: 1-57197-387-7
Library of Congress Control Number: 2003093080

Printed in the United States of America

This book honors the courageous ones in the history of human progress who defied religion's autocracy, the power structure. The reason, the logic, and the sacrifices of the courageous ones make it possible for freedom to evolve.

INTRODUCTION

Religion is frequently inherited. A parent or caretaker's beliefs are introduced early in a child's life, making the continuation of that belief almost a certainty. In addition to this early implant a child will later encounter peer pressure. That will be followed by the so-called tyranny of the masses. Conformity, or the status quo, is highly favored.

Although history, both national and world, is part of most academic studies, the history of religion is seldom included, at least not until the college and university level, when it is most likely an elective. Add to this that few people read the Bible, at least beyond passages recommended by a cleric, and you have the answer to why the public has almost no knowledge of the violence and deviant behavior of the biblical characters.

The purpose of this book is to review some of the biblical history and to call attention to the fact that religion constitutes a power structure, created and maintained for the purpose of controlling and exploiting the public. Religion's principal weapon is fear. In addition, religion is guilty of deception for alleging to be the source of peace, though its history is filled with wars, intrigue, and murder. A logical question is, how does religion maintain its support?

The reason is quite straightforward. Throughout history most humans have longed for peace, for a safe place to carry out their lives, but religion's mantra rather than history impacts the young mind. As Santayana eloquently stated, "Those who do not remember the past are condemned to repeat it." Hence, for millenniums religion has failed to bring peace. It is time to seek other means, and this book offers some alternatives.

YOUR HEALTH AND WEALTH
MAY BE IN DANGER

∽◯∾

If you happen upon a written work in which a talking snake is one of the principal characters, you have good reason to exercise extreme caution. In fact, it might be wise to take a guarded position, for this fable has been known to cause humans to become violent. Talking animals are often used in fables to portray a myth or legend. However, this particular story of a talking snake has caused some unusual human behavior. Usually fables or fairy tales are a pleasure to read because they project virtue or fair play. However, the interpretation of the talking snake story has caused some people to react irrationally, even to the point of killing one another. Examples include Northern Ireland, the Middle East, India, Sudan, and Nigeria, to name just a few trouble spots. Though this snake story has been around for centuries, the discourse has led to numerous interpretations and beliefs. Possibly the ease with which the story's meaning can be shaped and the many contradictions within the book creates problems. You probably have guessed; this caution is in reference to the Bible.

However, the snake is not the only talking creature in this book; the authors enhanced the fairy tale with a talking ass in Numbers 23:28–30. Just in case you prefer fish stories, the authors also covered that base with a real whopper in Jonah 1:17. It begins with the all-knowing, all-powerful Lord being unable to get Jonah's attention. Instead, the Lord uses a unique method of getting attention; he has a "great fish" swallow Jonah, then hold Jonah in the fish's belly for three days and three nights. We are not told how the Lord arranged for an accommodating great fish to be in the right spot at the right time to grab Jonah. Like any fairy tale, such as Snow White or Jack and the Beanstalk, one should not get concerned with details and spoil the story. After all, if the Lord is credited with creating fish he probably knew how to communicate with them. Some details do cause trouble, though—like knowing the species of this great fish. Then it appears that after three days and nights the fish either couldn't digest Jonah, or the fish received instructions from the Lord to vomit Jonah onto dry land. The Lord showed some consideration, because after that length of time Jonah surely needed dry land and some grass to clean off the fish's digestive juices before asking the Lord what this was all about.

This fairy tale might have been "swallowed" by ignorant peasants a few thousand years ago, but today people are unlikely to swallow it. For instance, today we know that only sperm whales have throats large enough to swallow humans and also that sperm whales do not exist in the Mediterranean Sea where biblical stories took place. The mouths of other whales are constructed with a bone-like baleen to strain out everything except the tiny sea creatures that constitute the diet of most whales. The really odd thing about this story is its similarity to an earlier Greek myth about Hercules, who also was swallowed by a fish and held in the fish's stomach for three days and nights. Do you suppose the divinely inspired writers copied— that they actually plagiarized—this ancient myth, even though they alleged to have been 'divinely inspired'?

It is also noteworthy that in Matthew 12:49 the authors who wrote about Jesus refer to this Old Testament fish story of Jonah. This detail is significant because nothing in the New Testament was written by Jesus, who apparently was illiterate. The authors of the New Testament had a vested interest in tying Jesus to the Old Testament. The New Testament did not exist until the fourth century, after a prolonged sorting and editing of stories about Jesus. Nearly four hundred years of storytelling and writing took place before the final draft was selected. In the completed draft the moral sentiment and gospels, which include the parables attributed to Jesus, follow the literature pattern of that time. The birth, death, and resurrection stories are typical of the myths of that time and are borrowed from the longstanding pagan religions that preceded the new religion.

The period represented by Old Testament stories took place before written languages were invented, making these stories the work of patriarchs who passed them along orally for centuries. Does it seem strange that an all-knowing, loving deity would omit having someone capable of writing in order to communicate and document his message to the people? Certainly this would have avoided a lot of misunderstanding. Instead, history shows that humans plodded along for millenniums with oral storytelling, gradually leaving some reference with petroglyphs, the pictorial symbols that preceded alphabets. The patriarchs and tribal kings orally passed stories along, which in time became legends. When writing was finally invented, old legends were recorded with all the additions and exaggerations of centuries of storytelling. Plagiarism and repetition were passed along from who knows where. However, ancient stories of revered leaders followed traditional formats, consisting of 1) a miracle birth, 2) tales of important victories and prophecies, and 3) a resurrection and ascension into heaven. The story of Jesus follows the common pattern of the era.

Today a reasoning, somewhat knowledgeable person would ask, "Why would an alleged all-knowing, all-powerful God have no better way to give his message to the world except to sacrifice a human who some religions claim to be his own son?" In storytelling it is safest to follow custom and tradition. The biblical story followed the existing pattern of the time. As for a human sacrifice, the Old Testament documents that the Lord approved of sacrificing the firstborn. In biblical parlance, what does another human sacrifice matter when tens of thousands were already killed by biblical heroes?

However, for a reasoning mind other lingering questions remain. Why would an alleged loving, all-powerful, and all-knowing deity select a backward, warring tribe in Israel to introduce a message to the world, when advanced civilizations existed in Greece and Babylon, as well as in Asia Minor? In fact, when the collection of biblical stories was finally put in writing, the stories show a distinct Asian influence, even adopting some parts of Asian religions. Another question: Why did God speak only to warriors, who plundered and killed? The warriors were the power structure, and a claim to be on speaking terms with God reinforced the authority to issue commands and threats of death to those who did not conform. In fact, God is a coconspirator in countless biblical stories of war and plunder. Another question: Why do believers pray to this deity to bring peace when the biblical history contains continuous war approved by God? Is something quite amiss in our human intelligence or our psyche? Faith and reason are clearly not compatible.

Christianity, as well as most religions, asks people to believe that a loving, all-powerful deity selected Jesus to give a message of peace to the world through a scheme that ends in bloodshed. The excuse religion devised for this unfortunate end was that Jesus died for the sins of others. Reason and logic are continually stretched. The message for our salvation was left to Jesus, who apparently could neither read nor write. In addition, no evidence shows that Jesus intended to start another religion. The biblical stories were written years, even several decades, after Jesus' death, mostly by people who did not personally know Jesus. The stories are therefore hearsay. The God in this story did not even have the foresight to have someone record and preserve something about the early life of Jesus. Is this the way to present a hand-picked person to bring a message to the world?

The ending turns out to be a typical political event, the kind that has occurred numerous times in history. An established power structure, in this case the Sadducees and the Pharisees, convinced the Roman administrator, Pilate, that Jesus was a troublemaker and a threat to the community, and that it would be in the government's best interest to help the established power structures get rid of this nuisance. Pilate hesitated, but being a typical politician, he reasoned that it was better to eliminate one troublemaker than to offend the dominant religious power structure. What we have is a story put together decades after the death of Jesus, by a few individuals who recognized that the lingering public support for a messiah could be used to start a new power structure. Even today Christianity lends itself to splinter groups that start new power structures.

Why would so many people claim to be believers of a story that very few people read and of which most people only remember the bits that a clerical power structure relates to them? To some extent the Bible is a smorgasbord, containing something for a wide assortment of tastes. If you prefer hunting to fishing, an unusual story is available for you in Judges 15:4–5. Samson gets the Lord's help in getting rid of the enemy Philistines. The Bible clearly establishes that the Lord prefers aggressors who like to kill. Samson used an unusual technique, employing the scorched-earth policy to punish the enemy. First Samson caught three hundred foxes, then tied the tails of a pair of foxes together, along with a combustible material called fire-brand (probably straw). Then Samson set the tails on fire, released the foxes that run through the Philistines' fields, burning the corn, vineyards, and olive groves belonging to the Philistines. We are never told what the Lord had against the Philistines, though it appears Samson wanted their land. God seems to help those who covet. The story also omits telling how Samson caught three hundred foxes or how he kept that many until ready to employ the trick of tying the tails of feisty, wild foxes together without getting bitten. How long would it take to catch and then hold three hundred foxes until ready to release them with burning tails? Samson was lucky; this barbaric era had no animal cruelty laws, and the Lord had no objections either. The Lord just wanted to be rid of the Philistines, though no reason is given. The Bible is declared to be the truth, written by divinely inspired individuals whose identity is never disclosed. In addition, the credibility of many of the stories requires a lot of faith.

The Samson story includes some interesting moral implications for a book alleged to be the model for humans and a family book. In the story, Samson's father gave Samson's wife to a friend. As you would expect, Samson became upset, though the story says he had been fighting with his wife. In spite of his family problems Samson continues to fight and kill Philistines for the Lord. The commandment "Thou shall not kill" apparently does not apply if God is in on the action. Samson was so successful in killing Philistines that he received the Spirit of the Lord. The nature of this reward is not explained; it may be similar to self-esteem. With this medal of honor, Samson used the jawbone of an ass to kill one thousand Philistines (guns, bombs, machetes, etc., had not been invented yet). Not only is the body count a nice round number, but the type of action Samson used would call for close, bloody encounters. One would really have to like that kind of vicious activity and feel comfort in the knowledge you were pleasing God.

All this action made Samson thirsty, so the Lord accommodated this heroic warrior by hollowing out the jawbone of an ass and making water appear to quench Samson's thirst. Do you believe it? The United States could use this kind of assistance from the Lord to search for and destroy al-Qaeda! The Samson story is not complete without a touch of sex, which apparently added interest for ancient as well as modern readers. Samson has a liaison with a harlot, and because the Bible is a family book you can explain this part to your children. Several other uplifting chapters in the book of Judges include sex if you care to pursue this further.

Because the Bible is declared to be the truth, your faith should not waver just because the Lord approved of murder, slavery, suppression of women, and a variety of roguish behavioral patterns that are not permitted today in developed nations. For some reason people continue to exhibit violent behavior where religious and ethnic differences exist, such as in Bosnia, Kosovo, Ireland, Egypt, Indonesia, Afghanistan, and elsewhere in the Middle East. For reasons that are hard to understand, after World War II the U.S. government became involved by giving major financial support, military technology, weapons, and troop training to almost anyone who asked for it. It is amazing that in wars and other conflicts, each side claims that God is on their side. However, the mythical deity has never lifted a finger to resolve these problems, even though the Bible stories do not lead one to believe God has ever taken a position of neutrality.

Believers of the biblical stories claim God offers a fountain of love, even though the Old Testament stories are mainly about wars, in which God communicates with the warriors, helping them to plan and conduct wars. As is customary today the enemies are always people who hold different beliefs. God takes a dim view of competition. A review of history shows that religion was frequently the cause of wars, which is also the case today. A possible explanation for this contradiction is that every group of people in the world—an agency, club, fraternal group, or a religion—always has an established power structure. Of course, power structures occur within most species, where dominance is often achieved by force. Power and greed are certainly dominant drives in humans. Along with power, humans usually desire to maintain the status quo, which means "Don't rock the boat." The major tool employed by power is fear, which happens to be the emotion capable of overriding all other emotions. Power and fear can really stir the adrenaline. Religion provides generous amounts of fear but is short on proof.

A dominant leader among humans will, of course, be surrounded by a supporting group that owes him or her allegiance and is therefore ready to defend and maintain the status quo. A leader also gains considerable help from the common human characteristic of resisting change. The status quo becomes hard to upset, guaranteeing that human progress will move slowly. The use of fear is not only the mainstay of religion, but fear is widely used to sell many ideas and types of merchandise. In the animal kingdom, a leader often has to overcome challengers in aggressive conflicts. However, the weaker one eventually withdraws. Humans are different, because they are one of few species that kill their own kind. Human leadership has often been determined by war, in addition to leaders frequently employing skullduggery, deceit, and character assassination.

Religious differences have killed many people in both small and full-scale wars. However, terrorism is a more recent form of killing and has been well demonstrated for about thirty years in Ireland, in the so-called Holy Land of Israel and Palestine, in the Hindu/Moslem mayhem in India, in the Christian/Moslem wars in Sudan, in the numerous islands of Indonesia; the list can go on and on. Following the terrorist attack on the World Trade Center in New York, the United States seems unable to understand why anyone would hate us. Rather than consider the possibility that we might be doing something that offends or irritates others, we choose to camouflage any such possibility with a liberal use of "God Bless America" banners and songs and a military response.

Isn't that the response found in the Bible? Here in the United States no one dared to ask the question, "Where was God when this terrorist act on the World Trade Center occurred?" It took years for terrorists to plan such violence, as did the bombing of the Federal Building in Oklahoma, yet no one received even a hint from God that a lot of people were going to get killed. Even the IRA in Ireland often alerted British officials that a bomb had been placed. The strength of a myth is always amazing, particularly when the brain has been trained to avoid reason.

Would it be out of character for an advanced nation, which we consider ourselves to be, to ask ourselves, "What could cause such hate to develop in such a large part of the world that it would create the terrorism that now threatens our security? Is it possible we have done something wrong? Did the animosity start with the Christian Crusades that took place about a thousand years ago? Did the Seven Sisters oil cartel's collusive agreements for oil leases with corrupt Arabic tribal leaders contribute to this distrust? Would jealousy, poverty, and lack of education lead to terrorist acts? Has our government support-ed corrupt, undemocratic regimes throughout the Arab world? Is the characterization of the "Ugly American" really valid? Have we ignored the Lincolnian idea of the danger to a nation that exists half free and half slave, which in our case applies to world conditions? Have we concentrated on delivering guns to almost anyone who asked, but ignored the need for education? Have we repeated the error of building military capabilities in countries that now threaten us? Is our military response to sup-press the unlimited pockets of dissent throughout the world the most effective, long-range tactic, though it fits biblical stories?"

LOOKING AT OURSELVES

❧⚬❧

Judaism and Christianity claim that humans are made in the image of God. This is intended as a complement, but it actually explains the source of human violence. Take a look at the record. Judging from Bible stories, God has a short fuse. Read Joshua 10:10 for example: "And the Lord discomfited them before Israel, and slew them with a great slaughter at Gibeon, and chased them along the way that goeth up to Bethhoron, and smote them to Azekah, and unto Makkedah." Joshua even got help from the Lord when he asked to have the Sun stand still so he could finish killing people that day. The story says the Lord complied, though science later determined the biblical error: the sun does not move! Check out Joshua 10:13: ". . . until the people had avenged themselves upon their enemies." Or take a peek at Joshua 8:1–8 where the Lord tells Joshua to make war on the Canaanites; no reason given, just do it. Or look at Joshua 8:25: "And so it was that all that fell that day, both men and women, were twelve thousand."

While you're at it look at the Lord's orders to Moses in the Numbers 25:4:"Take all the heads of the people and hang them up before the Lord against the sun, that the fierce anger of the Lord may be turned away from Israel." Hardly a compassionate God; combatants in modern warfare are urged to follow the Geneva rules rather than stoop to the level found in the Bible. Ponder, if you will, the revenge prescribed in the Bible. Take Numbers 35:19: "The revenger of blood himself shall slay the murderer: and when he meet him he shall slay him." Though this is contradictory to the Ten Commandments, Ecclesiastes 3:3 states: "There is a time to kill. . . ." But again, like a smorgasbord, you can pick and choose whatever fits your taste.

In analyzing the biblical claim that humans are made in the image of God, it is important to remember that people in biblical times did not have an inkling of the nature of the world around them. Violence and plunder were the common pursuits of every biblical leader, who of course were warlords. It would be quite natural for a leader to create myths for an excuse to cover and explain away the violent acts that were committed. By the time writing was invented and the biblical stories could be recorded, enough mythical gods existed to explain every misunderstanding or question about life. Myths served as a camouflage; myths were and still are the substitutes for knowledge. As Judaism and later Christianity expanded into new areas they incorporated the pagan myths that existed. The Bible lists no order of worship, and therefore worship services are a collection of customs, adopted over time, including those practiced by early pagans. The ornaments accompanying religious services had the aura of a mystic calling spirits or even inducing hypnotic dreams, illusions, or trances.

Among the ornaments used in religious services, the rosary is a symbol used in several religions, possibly for the purpose of committing the mind to a routine. Rosaries vary in design; the

Buddhist rosary in Tibet has 108 beads; in Korea, 110 beads; and in Japan, 112 beads. The Moslem rosary has 99 beads, one for each of the various names given to God, although the devout believer is allowed to substitute 99 repetitions of "God be praised," The standard Catholic rosary has 150 beads, divided into 15 decades by beads of a larger size. The origin of this practice is vague, but it may have come from ancient Eastern religions. The use of holy water, holy oils, and incense can be traced to ancient pagan religions. The prohibition of certain food was a common part of the lifestyle in religion of early aboriginal tribes. Maintaining certain restrictions is important in exercising control by the hierarchy over the uneducated masses. An ancient symbol that carried over into many religions, beginning long before Christianity, is the halo symbol for saints, which is believed to have originated with the Greeks. Communion was also a pagan practice that was adopted from other religions, and though progressing beyond ancient rites, the eating of bread to represent Jesus' body and drinking wine or grape juice as his blood carries a tinge of cannibalism.

How Old is the World?

∽o∽

According to Old Testament genealogy the world is about six thousand years old. This is not the only miscalculation of the Bible. Belief in a flat Earth is hard to dismiss, though the Bible is alleged to have been written by divinely inspired people. Most people now accept the scientific evidence of the world as being billions of years old. In addition, ample evidence shows that the human species has existed on earth for millions of years. The recent *Jurassic Park* film should have acquainted many with evolution on planet Earth, along with organic and inorganic changes, and give viewers some appreciation of how slow human progress has been. From science we have the evidence of the development of abundant plant and animal life during the Paleozoic, Cambrian, and Devonian periods, though these are not mentioned in the Bible. Of course, myth makers would find it impossible to inject something they do not know!

From history and archaeology we know early humans were illiterate, a condition that certainly leads to insecurity, distrust, and fear. The evidence indicates that if there was an allegedly loving and all-powerful deity, he actually abandoned his children. Clearly, ample evidence shows that humans existed in a primitive state of confusion and fear, without a clue to the world around them. Of course, ignorance is difficult to dispel, so early residents of the planet were prime subjects for myths, superstition, and control by charlatans. In all species the powerful, not necessarily the best, take control. A mythical deity provided power structures that controlled by employing fear and force. Myths and superstition could be turned into assets, not only for control but to also provide some comfort to the ignorant masses. Life was not easy. Even the few thinking people who gradually appeared on the scene, such as the early Greek Homer, could only ponder and guess what caused rain and wind, or why fruits fermented into wine. Some thought night was a sort of dark force that blotted out day, that insanity was caused by black air, and disease came from marsh gas. What a pitiful state for the mythical god to leave the human species.

Myths are not required to provide proof, so the biblical stories give power structures control and, in early times, the authority to take care of dissenters. To doubt was blasphemy punishable by death, according to the power structure. Not only were the biblical stories effective for controlling the uneducated ancients, but the same stories control a great many people today. Why would a loving deity allow such neglect and abuse? Today, in developed nations, parents who allowed their children to exist in such conditions would be charged and convicted of child neglect. Consider the indifference of a deity that allows, even today, an estimated six thousand people to die each day from using polluted water. A high percentage of these deaths are children. Observe, if you will, that the divinely inspired authors of the Bible make no mention of health, nutrition, or protection from disease. The word "bacteria" had not even been invented, but if you believe in the creation story, those bugs are also of His making. For thousands of years humans paid a dear price in misery, slavery, and brutality due to belief in a mythical deity that supported violent, aggressive power structures. Today, developed nations have corrected much of the brutality and suffering associated with the primitive, barbarous life of early humans, but only where education has replaced the omissions of religion. History shows that Christianity opposed education for centuries, even persecuting those found searching secretly for knowledge.

The Search for Knowledge

An example of the struggle for knowledge by early thinkers is Socrates, who was killed by his own countrymen. Socrates tried to raise the level of awareness by asking questions to make people think, to justify their beliefs. Like today, many people become irritated when asked to explain or justify their thoughts and beliefs. Socrates was considered more than just a nuisance; he was declared a threat to the youth of that day and was forced to drink poison. They did not have guns to eliminate him quickly, but they did the best they could to rid themselves of someone who was different. Pythagoras, another early thinker, was interested in mathematics. He is credited for his theory of the right triangle. Apparently his thoughts and curiosity also alarmed the power structure, and he was forced to flee for his life. The alleged loving deity did not show an interest in people wanting to advance knowledge. The biblical God spoke only with warriors.

Today we recognize that the level of intelligence among humans varies; not all minds are created equal. Why would an alleged loving deity create such a difference in the capability of humans? It certainly makes people unequal in earnings, in lifestyles, and in their satisfaction and happiness in life. Can you think of any human parents who would choose to have great variations in the intelligence and ability of their children if they had the power that religion claims is in God's grasp? To the credit of human persistence, we now know that in the pursuit of knowledge the human brain does grow with use, as do other parts of the body. Though the process is painstakingly slow it does appear that when a threshold level of intelligence is reached, a rapid advance is possible, as currently demonstrated in computer science, biotechnology, astronomy, and quantum theory, to name just a few subjects that humans have discovered on their own.

To advance beyond the flat Earth mentality of the Bible required courageous individuals, willing to risk defying the objections of religion's hierarchy. The reward to the world has been the knowledge capable of identifying the DNA of plants and animals and of opening potential benefits to humans everywhere. The creation myth about man made from dust hardly compares to knowing that the human genome consists of roughly three billion base pairs, the building blocks that make up the thirty thousand to forty thousand genes to provide specific body functions, or that the human brain contains 100 billion neurons. It took painstaking study for humans to discover molecules, atoms, protons, and neutrons. Why wouldn't a loving, all-knowing God mention the Periodic Table of elements, to give humans a start on the mineral and chemical elements on Earth? Loving parents go to great lengths to provide knowledge for their children; the mythical deity of the Bible provided commands and threats that power structures used to dominate and control vast numbers of the human race.

Science has gradually expanded human knowledge to serve and benefit health and longevity and to promote an economy that improves the human lifestyle. However, each new step tends to raise fear of the unknown, and many prefer the safety of the status quo. This stance is always safe for politicians, whose greatest fear is not being reelected. Selective breeding of plants and animals has been widely practiced except in humans, who are controlled by the biblical myth that encourages unlimited begetting. Ample evidence in nature shows that excessive production results in some plants and animals dying from lack of space and nutrients. Excessive birthrates plague many nations today; however, education can bring population and economic opportunity into balance. But religions dominate our government, prohibiting the knowledge that could save huge numbers of humans from poverty and illness, and yes, even reduce the causes for terrorism. In biblical times unlimited procreating was essential to supply the grunts for the brutal wars waged by the power structures that claimed approval by a mythical deity. Also, procreation was a male thing, and males dominated, as anyone reading the Bible knows.

Today we know that human reproduction amounts to a crapshoot involving thousands of genes with no telling what the nature and capabilities may be of the new offspring. We have made considerable progress in controlling and improving the raising of plants and animals. However, a religious myth prevents anything that restricts human reproduction. The world would benefit from a few more Albert Einsteins, Thomas Edisons, or Abraham Lincolns, to name just a few who made major contributions for everyone. If the natural bodies of plants and animals can duplicate themselves, where is the ethical violation? Plants have been cloned for years. Religion, whose premise is on shaky ground, demands that even the research on human reproduction be stopped for fear of jeopardizing the creation myth. It is well documented that when a nation's religion and politicians stop science and exploration, that country falls behind the rest of the world. Pioneering in science will continue, of course, but by nations now trying to catch up.

One annoying drag on human progress is the ease with which charlatans, the unscrupulous, and downright crooks victimized the unwary and too often occupy positions of power. More information for public consumption is needed to prevent entrapment by false propaganda and also to provide access to the qualifications of those seeking public office. In nature, species are equipped with instincts to guide their lives. Humans, on the other hand, require about two decades before the mind is capable of applying reason in making decisions. The ability to use reason is not automatic. It is estimated that a person does not attain good reasoning capability until about age twenty-three, and then only after a period of applying mature thought processes. A major handicap for humans is the long time required to reach maturity. This time lapse allows myths, ignorance, and the status quo imparted by parents, other adults, and peers to affect, even neutralize, an inquiring young mind. Quite often the youthful qualities of curiosity, testing, experimenting, and originality have been neutralized and disappear by early adulthood. As a result, human development is actually random, taking millennia to progress from the erroneous flat Earth concept of the Bible to the current realization of the world's great potential.

Not only have humans evolved slowly on Earth, but the species was handicapped for millennia by a lack of knowledge. The undeveloped brain that existed in early humans was no asset. In addition, the human species tends to be gullible and superstitious, with the possible misfortune of having a large ego. The assumption that humans are superior to other species may have a pagan origin, along with the claims to immortality, to which no proof exists. The belief in immortality was demonstrated in early religions by burying the dead with all sorts of tools and provisions to be used in the next world. Evidence shows that this belief resulted in servants being killed and buried with the honored or notorious one, with the expectation that the servants would continue their roles in the next world.

Modern Christianity includes some of these pagan trappings, including the belief in immortality; no proof, though, shows that humans are treated differently after death than any other creature. The promise of immortality was not mentioned in the Old Testament. This modern belief has created expensive and entrenched burial customs, capitalizing on the myths of religion. Numerous businesses also exploit religious beliefs. Occasionally Christianity feels obliged to try to disassociate itself from commercialism during the Christmas season. This is tongue in cheek piety, for business has indoctrinated the public into supporting Christmas with gift giving. Business is not about to depreciate a myth that contributes a major part of its trade and income.

KNOWLEDGE INCREASES POWER

✌︎o✌︎

Is there an alternative to the creation theory? Through science it is evident to the reasoning mind that we exist in a universe of extraordinary energy, though chaotic and continually changing. With the knowledge gained from experience and empirical verification, humans have solved and converted Earth's resources into productive use. Our knowledge is far from complete with regard to the extent and complexity of the forces in the universe. For example, consider the magnitude and precision of natural laws, so valuable and also so unforgiving. Consider the array of species, prehistoric and those currently present; the knowledge science has provided on the existence and demise of species; and the geological formation of Earth and its tectonic plates. Humans have accumulated knowledge on volcanic eruptions, their concomitant effect on climates, on species, and on the formations that make up Earth. Information available today confirms that creation is far more than the simple stories devised by ancient tribal leaders, who were ignorant, uninformed warlords but clever enough to claim to be on talking terms with a deity as a subterfuge to endorse murders, robbery, and oppression. For millions of years early humans were subjected and oppressed by the crafty, shrewd, or shaman-like leaders of power structures, who used myths and employed human sacrifices to instill fear into the masses.

In developed nations today, those with open minds recognize from history and science that for millennia myths supplied the support for religions and the associated power structures, allowing the masses to be oppressed and exploited. Even today, nations dominated by religion have not achieved the progress of secular nations. Nations dominated by religion are subject to more violence and often are controlled by corrupt hierarchies. Some contemporary nations verifying this observation are Sudan, the countries of the Middle East, and some central Asian countries. It is not hard to recognize that creative minds will not be permitted to exist where religious dogma administers thought control to suppress any challenge to its myths. The historic U.S. Constitution separates church and state, allowing science and the implementation of invention to raise the nation to world renown. However, that position is being threatened as religion now influences our legislators. Religious myths may reduce our enlightened and technical progress to the point that the U.S. leadership in science will be surpassed by enterprising third world nations.

Historically, Christianity always resisted education, beginning with its Judaic roots in the myth of forbidden fruit in Genesis. From the beginning, Christianity restricted the interpretation of the Bible to clerics, who generally were uneducated as well as superstitious. Finally, in the mid-fifteenth century Gutenberg of Germany broke religion's monopoly on thought with the invention of the movable-type printing press. The reduced cost of books made reading material affordable for many people. Gradually humans recognized that their species appeared on Earth as an ignorant animal species. The biblical myth provided no information for life, only commands to ensure control by the power structure. Of what use was the concept of a flat Earth and an erroneous solar theory except to hold the human species in ignorance and bondage for millennia? Little hope remained for reducing human suffering as long as science, particularly knowledge of anatomy, was prohibited by Christian leaders. Gradually a few courageous people gained knowledge of human anatomy by stealing cadavers and conducting research in secrecy.

From history and sciences, including archaeology, we know that wherever tribal units of humans lived, a religion with a power structure enforced commands of a mythical deity. Only the warlords spoke with deities, thus ensuring the power structure of approval for murder and conquest. Again, recall that biblical stories are hand-me-downs from patriarch to patriarch over hundreds, even thousands of years. Think of the trouble that would have been prevented if the alleged compassionate deity had given some human the thought to invent writing at the beginning of human history. The stories we do have amount to historical fiction. Of course, the plot was easy for the patriarchs to manage to achieve a desired outcome, because the stories were written long after the event. It was easy to make the story appear as a forecast of the future. This scam is understandable among the ignorant masses in ancient times; it is much harder to understand why people in developed nations continue to believe these myths, when information about our universe is available to all who wish to read. This verifies author George Santayana's observation, "Those who do not remember the past are condemned to repeat it." In ancient times people had no idea where or why they existed. Humans still do not have all the answers about life, but the knowledge available is far more accurate than the myth of creating man from dirt and woman out of man's rib. That myth supported male dominance but it was far from accurate. Today we know the Y chromosome in the male sperm does not change the female cell to a male until the second month after conception—hence the reason for breasts on males, which is something the divinely inspired authors or spin doctors missed because they knew nothing about anatomy when the creation myth was concocted. Today an informed, reasoning human recognizes the pleasure associated with challenges and the satisfaction of achievement as an important part of our life here on Earth. The myths planted by ancient, ignorant warlords in secrecy with a mythical deity who favored war, slavery, and abuse of women are not a plausible alternative to the freedom provided by democracy and its leadership in the world.

MYTHS CAN INFLUENCE A
NATION'S POLICIES

∽o∾

The story of the Israelite nation starts with Abraham, an aggressive warlord who intended to plunder, raid, and take all the land he could possibly conquer. As an ally, or accomplice in his life of crime, Abraham invented a deity, the Lord, who spoke only to Abraham and promised to give Abraham what he wanted—namely, all the land from the Nile to the Euphrates. Conveniently and generously the mythical deity promised that Abraham and his heirs would be leaders. Abraham did not get the job done in his lifetime, and so the patriarchs who made up these stories and kept them going for centuries had to continue the plot with Moses, later with Joshua, and then on to others. This same myth is currently the cause of the current "Holy Land" fiasco. Why is the United States involved in this illusion?

The United States is involved for several reasons. One reason is that the United States is also dominated by its own religious myth, Christianity, although the Jews rejected that cult early on. This rejection caused Paul and other promoters to settle for accepting pagan gentiles. The United States can hardly raise doubts about the myth of Abraham's deity promising the Israelis the territory currently under siege in the so-called Holy Land because the Israelis could also cast doubts on the mythical deity supporting the New Testament. Reason and justice should tell the U.S. government that rights to property should be determined by financial transfers represented by contracts and sales. The disputed Palestinian land could probably have been bought outright with the billions of dollars the U.S. government has given to Israel, but the history of religion has been to resort to war to acquire land, as the Bible clearly established in the Old Testament.

As early as 1626 the Dutch West India Co. acquired Manhattan Island, New York, by purchasing the land from the American Indians. The transfer of this property involved cloth, trinkets and sixty Dutch guilders, a total value estimated at twenty-four dollars. Peter Minuit, the Dutch colonial governor, used this legal method of transfer of title and it has stood the test of time. Later the British purchased the island from the Dutch in 1637. The U.S. government should recognize the error of supporting Israel's war to acquire Palestinian land. The United States made expensive social errors in taking land by force, beginning with the American Indians. After killing many American Indians in skirmishes and wars, the survivors were forced into reservations. Through mismanagement of the reservations and the dire social consequences that followed, the United States now faces a legal confrontation of having cheated the surviving heirs out of billions of dollars in compensation. A century or more has passed, and this questionable acquisition by the U.S. government continues to fester. The United States repeated this same mistake in acquiring Alaska. This issue was resolved in the 1970s when the U.S. government paid the native population of Alaska by deeding millions of acres of Alaska territory back to the native population. With this background in our own history it is hard to understand why the U.S. government supports the Israeli myth of the right to acquire land by force, particularly when it is only based on the word of an ancient warlord, who claimed that a mythical deity promised the land to Israel as a homeland. Of course, special interests enter into the picture. Contributions to candidates for U.S. Congress by vested interests in Israel and some Jewish citizens in the U.S. usually ensure the incumbents' victory, which is tantamount to a lifelong job. The moral and legal method of land acquisition is far removed from the biblical method of taking land by force, which history shows does not settle anything.

The Biblical Method of Land Acquisition

❧

What began as a myth by patriarchs of Israelite tribes thousands of years ago continues to this day in the same manner, employing war to acquire wealth and power. Although the method has proven to be a failure, Abraham's biblical conquest is repeated based upon the mythical Lord declaring the Jews to be his favorites. A reasoning person should recognize that friction is inevitable where force is employed. Historically the myth has also served as a penalty for the Hebrew religion. To the rest of the world, the arrogance and the conceit in believing in a deity that selects favorites has produced a continuing plague on the Jews.

The Old Testament is a long story continued by patriarchs to construct a continuing saga of battles, customs, and legends of Judaism in establishing a homeland. Historians today consider some of these stories to be true and some parts to be greatly exaggerated. It is strange that the biblical stories by an endless succession of patriarchs do not appear in the histories of other nations or groups. For instance, Egyptian history—which even recorded the diet and routines of pharaohs—makes no mention of the biblical stories, even those that supposedly took place in Egyptian territory.

At a much later time in history, the New Testament came into being, compiled from a collection of many stories. Some people proposed starting a new cult based on what they alleged to be the message of Jesus. It should be remembered that the New Testament stories were written decades after Jesus' death, by people not personally acquainted with him. As far as anyone can determine Jesus was illiterate, as were most people in that era. In addition, the New Testament does not mention Jesus suggesting or intending to start a new religion. The message of Jesus was typical of a reformer; he protested the corruption and oppression by established religion as well as the Roman occupation. The words credited to Jesus by others were objections to the poverty and oppression many people endured. The biblical authors claimed to be repeating Jesus' words by including quotes from the Old Testament and the reference to the coming of a messiah. Such a reference would certainly offer hope to the beleaguered masses. Jesus probably didn't consider starting a new religion, because he is quoted several times predicting that a messiah would appear within the lifetime of people then living, and that the Lord would then resolve the injustice that existed. Of course, this is just one of many inconsistencies found in the Bible. We also know numerous instances from history of desperate people following the glowing promise of a reformer or a zealot.

The biblical stories of Jesus were written decades after his death by opportunists hoping to start a new cult by capitalizing on the public interest Jesus generated as he condemned the abuse exercised by existing power structures. Jesus' bravery in speaking undoubtedly increased his support by the common person. This enthusiasm, or hope for a change, apparently continued for a time after Jesus' death and sparked opportunists to think of starting a new cult. One of these cult promoters was Paul. It appears he expected to win over dissident Jews who were unhappy with the established religions, the Sadducees and Pharisees, and their established power structures. However, Paul's hunch failed; the Jews rejected the new cult, and Paul and his few supporters turned to the pagan Gentiles. Though religion would have us believe Jesus was the son of God, his prediction that God would appear within the lifetime of those then living and would resolve all injustice seems to be an error in reading the tea leaves. Now, two thousand years later nothing has happened except that religious power structures have grown rich by selling the myth to those who do not know history or apply reason.

Today religious myths permeate many facets of life. Though scientific evidence refutes the creation theory, the religious power structures continue to maintain support for a mythical deity. The tyranny of the masses is an effective aid or tool that Spanish philosopher Ortega described when he said, "The masses crush everything in front of them." Isn't it strange that no nation ever went to war over a dispute regarding scientific discoveries and knowledge? Religion remains a prime subject in initiating wars and always claiming peace will follow. Many people buy the mantra that peace will arrive when the current war is completed. Victor Hugo (1820–1885) expressed his exasperation as follows: "No more armies, no more frontiers . . . The day will come when you will lay down your arms."

Unfortunately, Hugo's dream for the human race has yet to appear. Hugo's dream and the dreams of many can only materialize in an educated world. To make a realistic start toward this objective, developed nations need to begin by reallocating at least one-half of their current military budget to education for themselves and also for undeveloped nations. For the last fifty years of the twentieth century, the United States and Russia armed every Hottentot and dictator in the world, and we now stand amazed that our security has constantly decreased. The desires for peace have failed to organize. If there are any lobbyists for peace in Washington, their presence is but a whisper compared to the booming voice of special interests, the military-industrial complex, and other beneficiaries of war. Religions do not seem to care as long as chaplains are included in the military.

THE LONG, NARROW PATH

The road to knowledge is often desolate and difficult to follow. Knowledge and reason are essential to understanding the myths that prescribe death to doubters. Any hope for the human species lies with the courageous, the committed few who existed even in ancient times. An early advocate for wisdom, speaking some twenty-five hundred years ago, was Aeschylus, who stated, "For Zeus who guided man to think has laid down that wisdom comes through suffering." The hardy heroes of ancient times surely knew suffering as they defied power structures and sought answers to the bewildering world surrounding them. Initially only a few observant individuals asked questions, though they saw only a small part of the world. The sky was a particular mystery with its stars, comets, the Sun, and the Moon, a stimulant to the imagination and a place for dreams of escaping from a brutal life on Earth. Religion grew by exploiting fear of the unknown, by creating myths and persecuting doubters.

Gradually, over a thousand years or more, inquiring minds refuted religion's flat Earth belief, but at the price of life for some pioneers. However, as always has been the case, the slow, incremental increase in knowledge paved the way for our current scientific knowledge of cells, atoms, genes, and DNA, along with mechanical and electromagnetic achievements. This accumulated knowledge occurred in spite of religion's history of deterring, resisting, and penalizing those found searching for knowledge.

We now know that ancient humans existed for centuries at many different places on Earth, and that each group in its ignorance fell under the domination of some religious power structure. Each group of humans created myths to fill their black hole of ignorance. Myths could possibly be credited for serving as reinforcing glue at a time of great anxiety and superstition. Fortunately, a few individuals believed something was missing, and their curiosity resulted in progress. At some point religion recognized that the mythical deity needed an excuse for inaction when disasters occurred. A fall guy was needed to take the blame, and the devil was invented. Although the devil was also a myth, it satisfied many and to this day still serves as a crutch for a surprising number. The invention of this dual hierarchy, a two-entity power structure representing evil and good, was ingenious. It allowed the mythical God to be credited for positive happenings and the mythical devil to take the blame for negative ones. Still another excuse was needed for events that confounded available knowledge. Again religion came up with a cover-up—namely, "God acts in mysterious ways," meaning that humans are not privileged to understand some events. This pact of excuses has wide acceptance, though the logic compares to flipping coins, where heads God wins and tails you lose. However, science and an evolving education system have reduced much of our lack of understanding.

Determining Responsibility

~o~

The exact nature of the formation and development of the universe is still open to debate among scientists. Scientific theory continues to change when new evidence is discovered. The Judeo-Christian tradition, of course, continues to defend its creation myth. With the accumulation of data from various fields of science that includes archaeology, we now know that some biblical events occurred centuries before they were made part of the patriarch's stories. This is not surprising, because slow travel and communications made observing and reporting of events very difficult. How and when information was reported means the biblical stories could not be accurate, though believers maintain the authors were divinely inspired. The information on events could have been repeated numerous times before someone, usually a patriarch, included the happening in a story. Biblical stories therefore are in the class of historical novels, much as James Michener's historical novels such as *The Source, Centennial, The Covenant,* or *Hawaii.* Michener's work is delightful reading, offering a degree of history, gleaned from bits of news articles initially prepared by an early reporter, then developed into interesting historical fiction. In biblical stories, the patriarchs represented a special-interest group—namely, to provide a continuing story of a deity selecting the Israelites as his chosen people and promising them land for a home site. The history of any people has its ups and downs, with defeats and returns to power. The patriarchs telling the Israelite story interpreted defeats as punishments for sins and victories as rewards granted by their mythical deity. The central theme was always that the Israelites were God's chosen people. In other words, the patriarchs wrote history, their history.

RELIGION DEFENDS THE STATUS QUO

❧⊶o⊷❧

Religions tend to be totalitarian and at times have administered severe penalties and punishment for challenges to their dogma. The Vatican, for example, suppressed the mathematical and planetary discoveries of Copernicus, Kepler, and Galileo in the sixteenth century. Their discoveries had the potential to open the mystery of planetary orbits. Though suppressed by religion for a long time, this scientific truth eventually opened the study of physics and astronomy that led to space travel and the Hubble telescope. True to form, the Vatican's action was to protect the power structure's dogma of a flat Earth and maintain that Earth was the center of the universe. Copernicus's and Kepler's theories refuted religion's belief and showed Earth as just another planet revolving around the Sun. Copernicus was punished for his illuminating discovery; he was excommunication by the Vatican and his work put on a forbidden list. This scientific discovery was not removed from the Vatican's forbidden list until 1835, nearly two hundred years after the discovery. In the interim Martin Luther also helped to stonewall progress by declaring Copernicus "an upstart astrologer." Religion has been a real drag on progress and often inflicted great suffering on those who challenged the dogma.

What would the Vatican's religious power structure have been trying to protect? Some biblical views and religion's dogma certainly were not exemplary. For example, consider this Scripture from the Numbers 38:7: ". . . and they warred against the Midianites as the Lord commanded Moses, and they slew all the males." In 2 Kings 15:16 the action of the leader who kills his way to the top, without rebuke from God, is described as follows: ". . . [S]mote all; the women therein that were with child he ripped up." There is no doubt that violence was very effective in getting people's attention, because fear is a universal weapon for maintaining control. We are told Nazi Germany's knock on the door in the night was also very effective. Of course, the biblical leaders—namely, the warlords whom God spoke to—were in accord with the precedent set in Exodus 12:12 where the Lord says, "For I will pass through the land of Egypt this night, and will smite all the firstborn in the land of Egypt, both man and beast: and against all the gods of Egypt I will execute judgment: I am the Lord." If you translate this belief into present-day language, it compares with the Taliban's ill-starred campaign, which had its beginning in a religious seminary. The Taliban's early attacks were described as entering battle with a Qur'an in one hand and a gun in the other. They could count on no interference from God. The Taliban repeated much of what is found in the Old Testament— namely, violence gains power.

PUBLIC APATHY CAN BE CHANGED

❦

History shows that it takes ages for the public to react collectively to oppose violence. Public apathy allows power structures to gain control, although at any point in time they represent a numerical minority. It is also apparent that the people affected by a power structure seldom have a choice in the matter. Even when a choice of leaders is provided, the integrity and ethical qualities of the individuals are seldom carefully studied or even disclosed. A historical exception to public indifference is when King John of England was forced to sign the Magna Carta in 1215. Imagine the horrors that preceded this event, the punishment and torture endured for years until an aroused public reached the point of demanding and gaining the initial civil rights and political liberties we now enjoy. Note also that when advances occur in societal conduct, it was not the work of some god. Social progress occurs only when the general public will no longer tolerate injustice. This same evolutionary process gradually modified the oppressive, totalitarian views held by the clergy as they carried out the Spanish

Inquisition over a period of some three hundred years. As late as 1527 the Protestant reformer Balthasar Hubmaier and his wife were imprisoned in Vienna, charged with "heretical teachings." After refusing to recant, the Holy Roman Emperor Ferdinand I ordered Hubmaier burned at the stake and his wife drowned in the Danube (see the July 2002 issue of *National Geographic*). There is no evidence of a deity ever raising any objections to human brutality. The British governing system that evolved laid bare the brutality of church-state collusion during the Spanish Inquisition and the Thirty Years War in Europe. Again, the gain in personal freedom was not the work of a mythical god, but the result of public enlightenment that forced religion's power structures to end their abuses.

ABOVE THE LAW

❦

To introduce this subject, it might help to ponder the meaning in a portion of *The Immorality of the State,* written by Mikhail Bakun in 1870. This bit of political philosophy may describe the life of all power structures.

> *The supreme law of the State is self-preservation at any cost. All States, ever since they came to exist upon the earth, have been condemned to perpetual struggle—a struggle against their own populations, whom they oppress and ruin. A struggle against all foreign States, every one of which can be strong only if the others are weak. And since the States cannot hold their own in this struggle unless they constantly keep on augmenting their power against their own subjects as well as against other States, it follows that the supreme law of the State is the augmentation of its power to the detriment of liberty and external justice.*

Power structures tend to consider themselves above the law, reserving the right to use force to maintain control. The U.S. government justified, at least to itself, the action at Ruby Ridge,

Idaho, where FBI agents shot an unarmed teenage boy in the back and killed his mother as she stood in a doorway, holding an infant in her arms. Also, years after the end of the Vietnam War, the wartime Secretary of Defense admitted he and President Lyndon Johnson lied about the Tonkin Bay incident used to expand and continue that unpopular war. Fifty thousand U.S. soldiers lost their lives in that useless episode of a power structure out of control. Too, let's not forget the power structure of the IRS that with the help of Congress pretends to administer or interpret some ten thousand pages of regulations and loopholes. Some have described the IRS as the bag man for a profligate, free-spending Congress. The federal government's General Accounting Office (GAO) surveyed the IRS in 1999 and found 75 percent of the answers given to taxpayers were in error. Public apathy allows this abuse of power to be swept under the rug.

The power structure of our federal government finances a vast array of foreign endeavors that are questionable under a strict interpretation of our constitution. Power structures are perpetuated by court decisions also. In the 1890s the U.S. Supreme Court upheld the legality of "separate and equal school systems" in the southern states. It took another seventy years before another sitting court reversed that decision. Today the power structure of the U.S. government and its court system is again out of touch with public thought when it denies hopelessly ill and suffering citizens the right to choose to die with dignity. An overwhelming majority of the public favors euthanasia administered by doctors, but the collusion of church and state denies individuals that right.

The alleged divinely inspired Bible lists nothing to relieve the pain suffered by humans due to the diseases that are also part of the mythical God's creation, if you believe the biblical creation story. The alleged loving creator should also be held accountable for various defects and chemical deficiencies in the human body that cause pain and suffering for many people. However, any known relief from pain and cures for disease are the product of science, the field of knowledge that religion obstructed for centuries. Catholicism objected to any product that relieved pain in childbirth until around 1850. All improvements and gains to our human lifestyle came from study and trial and error to gain intelligence. When illness lingers before death, science provides the knowledge to relieve pain and assist human dignity with the ability to control bodily functions. Church and state collusion prohibits the freedom of choice to end life for the incurably ill.

Adding the word "democracy" does not remove the possibility that power structures usurp individual rights. Democracies also err in using undue and excessive power. A frequent technique of legislators is to restrict freedom of expression by requiring an insurmountable number of signatures on petitions to introduce referendums. This amounts to retaining the status quo for vested interests. Switzerland is one exception; a referendum there is easily made a part of the election process, allowing voters to decide on issues before they become law. The Swiss system has been criticized for allowing superfluous ideas to be used as a delaying tactic. An important facet of democracy is the need for deliberation rather than speed to allow the merits of proposed legislation to be adequately studied. Expediting action too often benefits special interests. To ensure good government the public must be constantly aware of the tendency for those in power to abuse individual rights.

Power structures frequently allow ruling hierarchies to create a self-perpetuating monopoly. The hierarchy then has control of its own salaries and the number of staff members, as well as the freedom to travel at public expense, set their own retirement and health care benefits that exceed those of most voters, and then impose whatever taxes are needed to cover all expenses. The right of public review or protest is ignored. In the political arena, voting districts are gerrymandered in the interest of the power structures, thereby turning campaigns into smoke and mirrors. Reelection is virtually ensured along with the continuation of a lifestyle far beyond that of most taxpayers. Judaism and Christianity created a power structure by declaring the Bible as the word of God, though it cannot be proven and is therefore hearsay. Judaism's power structure began with warlords alleging to speak or be guided by a mythical deity that approved the warlord's violence and territorial invasions. The warlords made their own rules, including their definition of blasphemy, which was punishable by death. To the mythical deity and the warlords the world was flat, and unfortunately some of that thinking still exists today.

An example of how ancient biblical beliefs continue to this day to inflict violence and injury upon people is the opinion of a Nigerian Appeals Court upholding the biblical death by stoning of a Nigerian woman accused of adultery (*The Economist* magazine, August 24, 2002). The sentence is Muslim biblical punishment reserved for women. No record indicates that any deity ever objected to this brutal, barbaric punishment or why it applies only to women. Education is the best solution to this dilemma.

The self-perpetuating power structures of major religions declare the Bible to be the truth and a model for human conduct. No one bothers to give thought to the possibility that the antiquated biblical rules were created by a power structure of ignorant, superstitious nomads. For example, the Bible calls for death by stoning for violating any one of seven of the Ten Commandments. Nor do the modern advocates for publicly displaying the Ten Commandments in schools and all public buildings show concern that the first four commandments apply only to Christianity and Judaism, or that they refer to acts that are not illegal in the United States. Six commandments are absolutes that an educated, developed society seldom follows.

Believers claim the Ten Commandments possess all that is needed for a just society, ignoring the inconsistency between the commandments and the action of the revered biblical characters. For example, King David is guilty of false witness, stealing, murder, adultery, and coveting. Can any word besides "covet" describe the Lord's collusion with both Abraham and Moses to take the land of Canaan by force? The list of violators of the commandment on coveting is long; it includes Moses, Joshua, Lot, Joseph, Aaron, and David's son Amnon who loved his sister and raped her. Also on this list are Jeru, Menahem, Saul, and Gideon. Belief that the Bible is a perfect guide for mankind can only be the result of (1) the person not reading the Bible or (2) the person being willing to carry out the power structure's command to avoid having to make decisions. The Bible raises no objections to human and animal sacrifices, to slavery, or to reducing women to the level of chattel. The Bible also approves of killing unruly children, selling daughters into slavery, and killing children for disrespecting their parents. Though the Bible lists burning incense before God as an abomination, this pagan practice of burning incense remains part of some religious services.

Though our Constitution sets forth the separation of church and state, many elected legislators try repeatedly to require posting the Ten Commandments in schools and other public buildings. These legislators certainly do not know the history of religious oppression in the Old World that prompted people to leave in droves for America. Nor do legislators recognize the oppression that exists today in countries where church and state are in collusion. Nowhere in the Bible does it call for public prayers. In fact, Jesus is reported to have called this the act of hypocrites. Clearly our political system has degenerated in understanding the historical results of catering to pressure groups. Why did the framers of our Constitution insert the protection from old-world religious oppression? Our political system is now managed by special interests that virtually guarantee lifetime tenure in an elected office.

The common political stance of an elected official is to avoid initiating anything and to wait until a situation is so bad that surveys show the public has already decided what action is needed. Public officials will assure any organized pressure group of their support even by putting their name on a bill, knowing that the bill will most likely die in committee. This kind of leadership validates the observation that "Given time, all government programs become disasters." While civilizations around the world continue to suffer from ill-conceived, corrupt, and oppressive governments, not one shred of evidence indicates that a loving, all-powerful God ever tried to correct or change an abusive, corrupt power structure. Of course, it should be evident that myths cannot act. The purpose of a myth is to instill fear, beginning in childhood and continuing through life.

Escaping Responsibility

∞

The Judeo-Christian creation story allows God to escape responsibility for countless numbers of diseases that exist throughout the world. Why would the alleged all-powerful, loving deity create a human body that frequently suffers from malfunctions of its organs and chemical imbalances and not offer one single remedy? Old wives' tales have made a greater contribution to health. A considerate, visionary creator, having designed a fragile body subject to frequent breakdowns, would have provided a far greater service if the deity had established a spare body parts' dispensary instead of the Bible, which consists of wars and threats. Only through tenacious plodding to relieve suffering have humans advanced their knowledge of science and are now able to repair and replace parts of the human body. Why would a compassionate deity allow the elderly to suffer the pain and indignity of the most debilitating diseases without a word to correct or alleviate the cause? Science made possible the replacement of joints, hearts, lungs, and kidneys, as well as pacemakers to supplement unreliable hearts. Where in the Bible can you find a caution that sunlight causes cancer or a suggested remedy or means of prevention? Care to guess how humans learned that certain plants, like mushrooms, are poisonous? What other species has a lifestyle that leads to obesity and drug addiction or that lives in squalor and filth that most species would reject? This question excludes pets kept by humans who abuse their pets and frequently themselves with excessive amounts of food and lack of exercise.

Humans had to discover and develop each field of science, such as biology, chemistry, geology, electromagnetism, and astronomy. To understand why Judaism and Christianity remain silent on the Bible's omissions of these essential fields of knowledge, one needs only to recognize the ignorance and superstition of people, including the patriarchs, in those primitive days. To believe in the divinely inspired authors of those stories is to lack the knowledge of history. None of the knowledge known today was revealed to anyone in biblical times or for centuries after. The Bible is simply a collection of stories that amount to a palliative, an excuse devised to fill the black hole of ignorance, to calm or mollify the insecurity of the uninformed masses. The resulting mystery warrants an indictment on human intelligence. That such a period of make-believe using myths could continue for so long and persist even today raises a cloud on educational systems.

ARE HUMANS GULLIBLE?

∽∘∾

Why do humans accept myths without question? Such acceptance may indicate a subconscious fear of the unknown, possibly contributing to the popularity of searching for roots. Is there something about the human mind that makes it easy to manipulate? Actually, the mind can suffer from a wide range of maladies that contribute to instability. The mind can be disoriented, have a short attention span, hallucinate, have flights of fancy, and suffer from schizophrenia, epilepsy, delirium, autism, illusions, ecstasy, and depression. In addition, detriments to mental stability include anger, ego, strokes, Parkinson's, Alzheimer's, and Lou Gehrig's disease, to name just a few common disorders. Is it any wonder that brainwashing is so easily accomplished and enduring? To all these destabilizing factors religion adds fear, the emotion that overrides all other emotions. Religion could be considered inherited since parents and peers pass along beliefs that may be unfounded and prejudiced. Will Rogers is credited with saying, "It's not what we don't know that is a problem; it's what we know that ain't so that gives us trouble."

Until a person achieves a reasonably good education, one that includes a fair understanding of the nature of the universe, life's problems can appear daunting. Cults and religion exploit insecurity by describing in word and pictures the dire consequences that meet those people who do not conform to and believe the mythical stories. Until the mind is capable of reason the myths of religion often fill the voids in some minds. This hardly explains the effect that fear and insecurity impose on the mind. For example, the Catholic sacrament of confession alleges that revealing some offensive act or thought to a cleric will clear the slate with the deity. Of course, the existence of the deity is based only upon faith and cannot be proven. As previously noted, mental frailty allows a person's mind to be manipulated and controlled by fiction. Religious power structures capitalize on this frailty and the insecurity that is commonly sensed in life. Religions gloss over that the mythical deity spoke only with aggressive warlords, murderers, and deviates. These unsavory characters concocted stories to cover their plunder, violence, and coveting the property of others. Because few people read the Bible, they are unaware that the mythical deity was a coconspirator with the warlords' criminal acts.

Christianity does not mention that Jesus reminded people they did not need clerics to intervene and that people could speak directly to their God. Keep in mind that Jesus never mentioned starting a new religion and that his described role was more of a reformer. He objected to oppression by established religions as well as Roman domination. The established religions of Jesus' time, just as today, wanted financial support for acting as the intermediary between people and God. If people followed Jesus' message, the religious power structure would wither on the vine. No wonder the religious hierarchy, the power structure, pressured Pilate to eliminate Jesus, the troublemaker.

The history of religion shows that abuses by clerics were common, including the Vatican's sale of indulgences. The moral travesty within the Vatican was so flagrant that Martin Luther, a monk in the Order of St. Augustine, posted his Ninety-five Theses on the church door in Wittenburg, Germany, and founded the Lutheran denomination. To gain an insight into this subject, read the book *Papal Sins* by Garry Wills. Again, those who do not know history are condemned to repeat it. Today people continue to financially support clerics and their grand edifices, perhaps believing that these contributions make them religious. Contrary to Jesus' explanation, many people go right on paying clerics to pray for them.

As young people are introduced to religion, no one mentions to them religion's long history of abuses of power, religion's belief in a flat Earth, its centuries-long obstruction of education, or religion's execution of persons holding different views of the world. Nor is the Bible explained as a document of prohibitions, requiring obedience to a deity that conspired with murderers. Christianity contends the Bible was written by divinely inspired persons and has severely punished those who doubted or expressed disbelief. Religion falsely illustrated with frightening pictures of what would happen to nonbelievers. No one mentions that the biblical stories were written by people with no firsthand knowledge of Jesus. The biblical writers were the modern equivalent of spin doctors with a vested interest. Religion does not dwell on historical facts. For example, the contents of the New Testament were not decided upon until the fourth century, at the Council of Nicaea in 325 C.E. The final selection came after considerable sorting, winnowing, and editing of many stories; the final draft did not appear until 367C.E.

The final draft of the New Testament includes twenty-seven books. Christianity does not point out that none of the writings are the actual words of Jesus, or even eyewitnesses to Jesus. Even the authorship of the Gospels of Mark, Matthew, Luke, and John is uncertain. The stories of these four principle books also vary. Only the Gospel of Matthew refers to the Lord's Prayer and the Sermon on the Mount. The Gospel of Mark does not mention the birth of Jesus but starts with the adult Jesus being baptized by John the Baptist, who tried to convince Jesus to be a preacher. Why was John the Baptist's counseling needed if Jesus was the son of God? In Luke 14:26 Jesus is reported to have said, "If any man come to me, and does not hate his own father and mother and wife and children and brother and sisters, yes, and even his own life, he cannot be my disciple." Throughout the stories about Jesus the word "family" is never mentioned. Numerous inconsistencies exist within the Scriptures, and the miracles credited to Jesus are also found in the Old Testament.

Believers in religion tend to strongly oppose homosexuality as a violation of the word of God. Oddly though, an inference in Mark 14:51–52 raises the question: Why would this incident be included in the story of Jesus? The inclusion reads as follows: "And there followed him a certain young man, having a linen cloth cast about his naked body; and they laid hold on him." The next verse reads, "And he left the cloth and fled from them naked." On this same subject, Judges 19:22–24 also alludes to homosexuality. A logical question is, why would an allegedly loving and all-powerful God create humans with behavior characteristics that cause believers to consider certain acts as deviate and sinful?

COMPARING THE OLD AND THE NEW

∽o∾

Of course, the element of time makes for a striking differ-ence in the writing style between the Old and the New Testaments. The latter particularly places less emphasis on God and his warlords engaged in murder, plunder, and coveting the land of others, or the deviate behavior of his henchmen. The New Testament stories give more attention to the preferences of ordinary humans rather than warlords. Did someone finally get to God or the spin doctors? An analysis indicates a moral sentiment invading the writing of the spin doctors, a trend toward the society of developed, stronger nations, such as Rome. Historically cults were numerous but usually tolerant of each other. The parables credited to Jesus and also found in the Old Testament were probably intended to show a link between the old and the new. The story of Jesus' birth, death, and resur-rection follows the pattern of the common myths of that time and were part of pagan religions.

NOT MUCH CHANGES

The biblical stories are representative of human history that to a great extent is about war or the preparation for war. Though aggression is an innate characteristic of humans, this less than desirable trait is not addressed as prompting the violence in the Bible. The Old Testament's purpose is to construct the story of God's selection of the Israelites as his favorite people. The New Testament's purpose is to introduce a new cult that later becomes Christianity. One has to be searching and be willing to apply faith, because the story follows the typical birth, a short message, then the death of the principal character, which is the pattern of all mythical leaders at that period of history. The beginning of Islam that took place about 600 C.E. is also quite similar.

In comparing the Old Testament and New Testament stories, the old extends over a longer period of time, during which patriarchs orally passed along their story, but maintained the objective of a deity selecting the Israelites as his favorite people.

Regardless of the outcome of the travails of life, the patriarchs kept the thread of a deity always guiding the Israelites to their ultimate goal. If along the way the Israelites were defeated by an enemy power, the story alleged it was the Jewish God's way of punishment for sin. Following any defeat, there is the plot of revenge and finally a resurgence of Israel's power. The return to power was always the reward granted by the deity. The problem with this biblical history, though it follows the normal reaction of the human species, is the failure to recognize a basic law of the universe. That law is that for every action there is an equal and opposite reaction. That is why war has not and cannot produce peace. Even today, very few people understand that this physical law of the universe is equally true and applicable to human behavior.

Throughout the Bible the ethical response is an eye for an eye, etc. Education is the only means of correcting this human fallacy, and it should be remembered that religion opposed education for centuries. This change in human behavior is quite well accepted in developed nations, though aggressive acts still do occur. If a loving deity did exist, why do humans have this animalistic aggression, willing to kill and oppress others? Of course, religion alleges that man is made in the image of God, and with the Bible involving God in murder, revenge, and oppression of women, man has all the characteristics of the deity that created him. This should be no surprise because it describes the actions of humans in the stories of Abraham, Moses, and other warlords. Religions would seem to serve a greater purpose if they accepted the responsibility to explore and understand the psychology of human behavior rather than uphold myths condoning human acts of mass murder, intrigue, and incest. Actually, Judaism's covetous deity would today be brought before criminal courts to stand trial for aggression against humanity.

Although it appears that the rank-and-file of the human race has always longed for a peaceful world, several persistent factors delay or inhibit this dream. One inhibiting factor is that we are just beginning to recognize the nature of our chaotic, constantly changing universe. As participants in or observers of randomly occurring events in the universe, humans have needed to learn to cope in order to exist. No deity since biblical times ever forewarned humans of earthquakes, hurricanes, or floods. Instead early humans were led to believe in a flat Earth and also erroneously declared Earth as the center of the universe. Science expands our knowledge of our universe, as well as our chemical, biological, and electrical constituents. How can one compare the Dark Ages and religion's role in oppressing knowledge with modern events like the recent discovery by astronomers of a quasar six billion light years away, dubbed PKS 0637-752, that radiates with the power of ten trillion suns? Or try to compare the reign of religion with our current knowledge of the cosmos that speeds forward aided by science with telescope mirrors perfected to the smoothness of a few atoms.

Freed from religious oppression and dogma we now know that our planet has changed dramatically over billions of years and that it continues to change. We are able to discern the possibility of global warming and assemble data to evaluate how much may be man-made and what may be due to climactic changes that occur over very long periods of time. The human lifetime is not long enough to accurately detect slowly occurring changes. Therefore, humans apply broad fields of science to accumulate data to help future generations with this subject. Our industrial/commercial/agricultural base and our lifestyle may have little effect other than on human activities and health problems. Much remains to be understood about the macro and micro impacts on Earth. Freed from religious dogma and oppression, our knowledge now increases constantly, whereas for millennia while myths controlled, humans made no improvements in their lifestyles.

A CLOSER LOOK AT THE PAST

～o～

Any story that claims to have the true explanation of creation but ignores the subject of health and avoids responsibility for creating a never-ending number of diseases without suggesting one remedy is probably hiding something. For instance, why isn't the meaning and purpose of life addressed in the Bible? How much trust should be given to a story of a deity that declares one power group, the Israelites, to be his favorites? Broken down to family size, what would children think of a father who declared one child as his favorite? Even worse, for a comparison, the prejudiced father would not bother to tell all his children of his decision but would allow his favorite child to boast and incite violence. Even though the biblical claim is hearsay, the story has created resentment and hostility throughout the world that endures to this day. In a nutshell, the Old Testament is a collection of stories by tribal patriarchs to establish a power structure. The mythical deity in the Bible, like the father in the example described above, is guilty of portraying egotism and promoting the continual warfare that plagues our planet. From the very beginning the biblical story is a ruse designed by a power structure to control others.

According to the writers of the biblical story, Jesus accused the established religion and the government of Rome of ignoring the poverty and suffering endured by the common people. Because Jesus' message touched the nerve center of the power structures, he was eliminated. The public dissent credited to Jesus' message apparently continued for some time after his death. This lingering dissent attracted special or vested interests into capitalizing by proposing new cults. As noted before, promoters of at least one of the new cults hoped to attract Jews who believed their established religion was oppressing the common people. However, the new cult leaders guessed wrong; the new cult did not appeal to the Jews and the promoters then made their pitch to Gentiles, the pagans. This outreach program to recruit Gentiles resulted in the new cult adopting pagan beliefs and rituals into religious services. One of the old established religion's policies was retained by the new cult—that of declaring doubters as heretics, or blasphemers, punished by stoning to death. The loving, all-powerful deity raised no objections. Have you thought about the hate and commitment needed to murder someone by stoning to death, particularly when done by a group claiming to promote love and peace?

That question can be extended, because history shows that the cult which evolved into Christianity practiced more than just moral persuasion to win converts. Later in its history the Vatican's Christian armies carried out the Crusades, from the eleventh to the thirteenth centuries, in order to eliminate Muslim infidels. This early program of ethnic cleansing by Christians was also used to eliminate the Moors and Jews in Spain during the fourteenth century, which was an early stage of the Spanish Inquisition. There is something mentally wrenching about burning people at the stake, the punishment used by Christian clerics and believers against those with different beliefs. As usual, the practice received no rebuke or condemnation from this religion's mythical deity. Unless you read history, you are probably unaware that cults and religions existed in large numbers prior to Christianity and generally were tolerant of each other. Christianity and other organized religions put an end to tolerance.

WHEN POWER STRUCTURES COMBINE

∽◦∾

As Christianity's power structure gained strength in numbers it moved to increase its influence by colluding with the government. The reinforced power structure of church and state resembles the ancient collusion of a tribal chief and the medicine man; between the two anything was possible. Church-state collusion also increased Christianity's economic and political strength, though biblical writers quote Jesus as saying, "Render unto Caesar those things that are Caesar's." That is not the only biblical comment ignored by organized religion. By colluding with government, religion became exempt from taxes and could tap the public treasury for financial support. Again, if you do not know history you are destined to repeat it. You may also forget that there are always two sides to a coin. History shows that when religion and government collude, the unforeseen and unintended consequences are that the government subverts and controls religion.

In preparing the Constitution the founders of the United States were aware of the oppression from a collusive arrangement of church and state. The founders were aware that after a period of Puritanism in England and twenty years of heated arguments over conflicts about religion and state, the English parliament in 1659 recognized that religion should remain free and that church and state must be separate. The founders heeded this history of church and state conflicts and included the separation of these powers in our Constitution, making the United States the first nation ever to do so. Today, religious and elected officials do not know their history, and both are about to prove that history does indeed repeat itself.

Few people realize that the Christian church was not a united power structure until after the Council of Nicaea in 325 C.E. At that time the four official Gospels of Matthew, Mark, Luke, and John were adopted. This decree brought an end to doctrinal disputes within Christianity about inconsistencies within myths that for several centuries had stirred real conflicts. Constantine I (280–337) was a contemporary of this period and shared in governing the divided remnants of the old Roman Empire. Control of these divided areas was difficult due to jealousies and disputes. One adversary of Constantine was Licinius, governor of a separate area of the old Roman Empire, who persecuted early Christians. This persecution prompted Constantine to compete by offering freedom of worship. At this time a popular religion or cult called Mithras also existed. Mithras was of eastern origin with longstanding practices in worship and administrative hierarchy. These practices were copied by the early Christian cult and remain part of Christianity's dogma today.

In 324 Licinius was defeated in a battle, and Constantine became emperor over the area that included Rome. By 330 Constantinople had become the new Rome. Christianity likes to claim Constantine as a believer, though he did not accept baptism until he was on his deathbed. Christianity has a convenient provision that, regardless of one's beliefs or behavior during life, a statement of belief by the dying person is sufficient to be admitted to Christianity and thus to heaven. Before Constantine died he used Christianity to consolidate his political power by outlawing other beliefs. His personal life emulates that of other biblical warriors; he killed one of his wives and also a son. Christianity does not point out that Constantine was the bastard son of a Roman soldier and a barmaid. Christianity does not mention his personal life, nor does it find fault with other murderers in biblical stories who colluded with God to succeed in taking the land and possessions of others.

Many historical events go unnoticed. History is written by winners, so the sordid side is often omitted. In addition, for centuries communications were so difficult that much information fell through the cracks and remains unknown to vast numbers of people. The impact of human actions can take decades to materialize. By the time an error is recognized, no one wants the pain of interrupting the status quo. The knowledge of the past easily escapes the current promoters of a special interest, because they usually have little to gain by digging into history. Neglect can also penalize, making the oft-quoted words of author George Santayana so appropriate: "Those who cannot remember the past are condemned to repeat it."

GOD'S OMISSIONS

❧

Though plagues and disease have at times decimated human populations as well as other species, no god has ever stepped forth with remedies or information to combat any malady. This should not be surprising, for what power does a myth possess other than to induce fear, which when combined with ignorance reinforces the power structures? A myth contains only the knowledge and characteristics of the person who spawns or initiates it. This explains the vengeance, hate, and brutality of the human species in the biblical stories. The biblical tribes that started and then maintained the myths knew nothing about the world that surrounded them, including anything pertaining to health. Only beginning in 1881, when Louis Pasteur proved his discovery of germs and contagion as the cause of illness, did humans have an inkling of the world of microbes and viruses. Naturally, Pasteur's new theory met solid opposition, even from medical doctors of that time. It is natural for humans to defend their beliefs, even though they are ultimately proven wrong. In 1879 Pasteur was denounced by members of the Paris Academy of Medicine for disputing the medical profession's belief that "miasm" (the doctors' term) was the cause of women dying in childbirth. Pasteur charged that doctors were the carriers of microbes and germs from the sick to healthy women, causing their deaths. Yes, the doctors pooh-poohed this chemist in their ranks, and no deity came to Pasteur's defense.

To prove his point to the so-called medical profession, Pasteur demonstrated his germ theory using anthrax, a germ widely scattered around the globe that remains a serious threat to humans and animals today. Pasteur successfully demonstrated his theory using sheep, but doubts continued in the medical profession for a number of years. As the germ theory gradually gained acceptance, the need for sanitation took the forefront, and cleanliness can now be credited for much of the increase in human longevity. Robert Koch (a contemporary of Pasteur), who was a country physician in Germany, was also exploring the germ theory. Both men are credited for the advances that came in medical science and the reduction of such epidemics as cholera and tuberculosis. Though millions of people died over thousands of years because of ignorance, not a word or tip ever came from a mythical deity. Even today the World Health Organization estimates three thousand people die every day from malaria, and that 70 percent of those deaths are children. Where is the loving God? Even today a vast number of human deaths are the result of polluted water. Billions of the world's people do not have access to a safe and adequate water supply. Why does religion hesitate to challenge the biblical myth on unlimited procreation when at least one fifth of the population is relegated to misery and an early death due to ignorance about health? Education, which religion suppressed for centuries, will provide the answers for health and population.

To be effective a myth needs a lot of protection from charges of inaction and failure. When the top person or entity does not act or live up to expectations, a scapegoat has to be invented. The early Greek and Roman myths invented numerous entities, enough to substitute for lots of ignorance and divert responsibility or blame. It always helps to have a fall guy. Therefore, Christianity and contemporary religions created another myth; the devil became the fall guy for the deity's failures. For instance, consider the corruption and dishonesty prevalent in government, business, and numerous daily human activities. Many of these corrupt and improper acts often escape conviction. Religion does not want God accused of neglect, oversight, or inaction on these matters. Thus, a catch-all punishment was invented; punishment is alleged to be meted out in an afterlife. With no feedback possible, that excuse is foolproof. There does seem to be a questionable relationship in the Bible where God and Satan talk to each other (Job 1: 6-8). Have they divided territory like the Mafia?

Owning a Bible seems to imply some redeeming feature, though no proof exists that the contents can be transferred to the human brain by osmosis, magnetism, or voodoo. To understand the Bible it must be read, though a thoughtful person is likely to be turned off. Granted, life is much easier if one accepts the majority view on any subject. Early in life we learn that it is dangerous to express different views, particularly about religion. Besides, it takes a lot of time and effort to gain enough information to form an independent opinion. Then one has to have the courage to express a private opinion. Accepting the majority view reduces the hassle and ensures that the status quo will go on and on. The Bible is the power structure's handbook for institutionalizing fear, an essential factor for control.

EVOLUTION IN ACTION

❧❧❧

A lot of knowledge is gained through trial and error, commonly referred to as the "school of hard knocks." A fair amount of scientific knowledge has also been gained by this route, as well as by pure accident. However, the statement attributed to Pasteur that "chance favors only the prepared mind" seems accurate. In the very early days of science, the information gathered was often fractured or incomplete, making the accumulation of the knowledge a slow process. Knowledge began to accumulate when curious, primitive humans began to ask questions. One of those inquiring minds was Pythagoras, born about 570 B.C. His curiosity eventually introduced the equation of the right triangle. Socrates, born about 400 B.C., is remembered for his philosophical reasoning. In general, a state of ignorance prevailed long before the biblical stories were transferred from a legend passed on by patriarchs into a written document.

Centuries passed before enough knowledge accumulated and was distributed widely enough to bring changes to prevailing lifestyles. Then, as now, resistance to change existed.

Religion has always had to protect its creation myth, making the clerics very edgy about people who dabbled in science. This fear is evident even today in religious opposition to stem cell research and cloning, though hybridization did slip by. As for cloning, what would be wrong with a few more outstanding scientists, inventors, or people like Bill Gates, people who have benefited the human race? Unless science is allowed to pursue the search for knowledge of the universe, human progress will be stopped in its tracks.

The advance in medical science we now enjoy is due to the bravery and curiosity of a few early pioneers that defied oppressive religion. Consider Giordano Bruno who in 1600 C.E. was deemed a threat to religion's power structure. He was declared a heretic and burned at the stake. In early life Bruno had rejected religion, fled from a monastery, then traveled for some fifteen years to evade punishment by religion. The Inquisition eventually discovered him in Naples. When he refused to recant his claim that an infinite number of worlds existed in the universe, he was burned at the stake on February 16, 1600. Galileo, another early pioneer, was forced to kneel before the Inquisition Tribunal of Rome in 1633 and renounce his belief in the Copernican and Kepler planetary theories. Until this time religion held that Earth was the center of the universe. Galileo was held in house arrest until his death. When a power structure is supported by myths, it cannot take chances on the spread of facts and knowledge. The modern conundrum is how so many people believe in religion when it is founded on myths and whose history includes murder and suppression?

A MAN'S WORLD

∽o∾

Women's loyalty to religion is equally hard to understand. For example, the Bible places women at the level of chattel, the equivalent of breeding stock to produce the grunts for the power structure's wars. The New Testament calls for silencing women. Check out Ephesians 5:24: ". . . let the wives be to their own husbands on everything." Then see 1 Corinthians 14:34–35: "Let your wives keep silence in the church. And if they will learn anything let them ask of their husbands at home, for it is a shame for women to speak in the church." Or 1 Timothy 2:12, another no-brainer: "But I suffer not a woman to teach, nor to usurp authority over the man, but to be in silence." Let's face it; the Taliban might as well have taken its lesson from the Bible on this subject! Commands to reduce women to chattel are repeated many times in the Bible, probably to make sure it was understood. Neither Jesus nor the apostles in the New Testament raised objections to this degraded status for women. In fact, Jesus is never quoted as mentioning the word "family." Even today, in many countries women are treated as second-class citizens or less, and religion is not demanding that this injustice be corrected. The Vatican, as well as some other flat-Earth mentalities, refuse to accept equal rights for women, particularly their right to control their bodies. This injustice is a major factor to a host of world problems that remain unsolved, such as education, overpopulation, welfare, employment opportunities, rising social costs, health, economics, and the environment. Again, ignorance is on the side of religion.

Slavery is another selfish and immoral practice condoned in the Bible. Until the time of the Civil War involuntary servitude was accepted by most religions in the United States. Today the religions that follow closest to their Holy Scriptures are those most oppressive of human rights. Take a look at religion in Iran, Iraq, Saudi Arabia, Sudan, Egypt, and Afghanistan; even the Israeli government resembles a theocracy. Currently in the United States some religious denominations apply pressure to state and national legislative bodies to the extent it is conceivable the United States could soon be added to the above list of backward nations. The power structure of the religious right in the United States, though a minority in actual numbers, is able to hold the majority of the population hostage, because elected officials pander to all organized pressure groups. The unorganized majority does not seem concerned that historically a church-state alliance increases militancy, suppresses ingenuity and freedom, becomes corrupted by government, and ultimately results in the withering of democracy.

Because so few people read the Bible, they do not recognize that the biblical stories were written during and for an era of uneducated, superstitious people who accepted myths as a substitute for knowledge. That many people in developed nations still believe in illusions and superstition is amazing. The allegedly divinely inspired authors of the biblical stories were the spin doctors for the power structure that kept belief in the flat Earth alive. We know today that wherever humans existed they concocted a creation story and frequently had their popular idols ascend into the sky after death. In a period of ignorance and superstition, myths may have served to calm feelings of insecurity held by the public in a rough-and-tumble world. However, the abuses by the power structure offset any possible benefit from myths. Of course, one should recognize the wisdom of numbers and knowing when to follow the herd to gain public acceptance.

RELIGION ADOPTS PUBLIC RELATIONS

⋙⟐⟐⋘

Contemporary pictures of Jesus exemplify a model of customized male grooming that an elite barber salon would use. Christianity chose to be realistic, for how much public appeal would there be for a Jesus depicted as a sweaty and dusty, a footsore pedestrian who considered foot-washing to be the ultimate creature comfort? As for Mary, Jesus' mother, Christianity has upgraded her to the beauty and charm of a Barbie doll. Why not? Does anyone complain about this modernized, make-believe, enhanced beauty? Beyond a doubt this upgrade makes the product easier to sell, compared to showing a scruffy, unwashed person, bent, barefoot, in tattered, dusty clothing. Truth in advertising does not apply here. With no format set down from on high, Christianity is free to satisfy local customs and conditions, and did so even to convert pagans.

What we now consider a developed nation is the product of educational and judicial systems that set guidelines for the interaction of humans. The authoritarian control held by religion for centuries was forced to moderate and accept the social changes demanded by an informed public. Christianity's Achilles heel was and still is education. The catalyst that opened the door to change was Gutenberg's invention of the moveable-type printing press about the mid-fifteenth century. This invention weakened the monopoly held by Christianity's power structure. The Bible was one of the first books printed with the new moveable-type press. As production cost fell on all printed material, common folk could own and interpret the Bible for themselves. Prior to this event, Christianity allowed only clerics to interpret the Bible. Gutenberg's invention initiated the beginning of the end to thought control by religion. Common people were eager for knowledge, and reduced printing costs gave them access to books. A knowledgeable and reasoning public ultimately produced what is referred to as the Enlightenment. By the nineteenth century, intellectuals like Robert Ingersoll, a Civil War veteran and later an attorney and an eloquent speaker, contributed greatly to bringing an end to the hellfire, brimstone, and fear that dominated Christianity and clerical sermons. However, remnants of old conservative religion continue in odd places. Just try to find a book by Robert Ingersoll in almost any public library. Religion continues to censor history.

REVIEWING BIBLICAL HISTORY

～o～

Few opportunities existed in biblical times to prosper and to gain wealth. The tools, skills, and material for crafts and manufacturing were not readily available. Today people recognize that poverty and ignorance can turn people to crime, but this was always a fact of life. In biblical times business ventures or opportunities to acquire wealth were scarce, existing mainly in population centers bordering the Mediterranean Sea. For the nomads—the tribes described in the biblical stories—life was characterized by dire poverty. The best way to acquire wealth was to recruit an army and invade other tribes. The rewards from plunder might be trinkets, food, livestock, and victims who could be sold as slaves. The Bible stories support these exploits by the leading warriors, justifying and enhancing their trade by claiming to be on speaking terms with the deity. A life of crime was really the top of the order.

No doubt about it, the God of the Bible loved armies; he was the myth a warlord used to justify crime. Of course, history is written by winners, so the biblical stories—told, retold, and freely embellished for centuries—are comparable to the ethics of Jesse James, John Dillinger, and other gangland heroes. When writing was invented, the legends that existed were set down and, as expected, they endorsed the vested interests. Whether the biblical stories were orally repeated by patriarchs or written made little difference to the uneducated, the superstitious. Life fit the description of "nasty, brutish, and short." Without courts or laws, the rules were laid down by whoever happened to be in power. Imagine living where warriors claim the support of a deity and parade around with a victim's head on a stick, as noted in the Bible! The rank-and-file person had little choice. The biblical God spoke only to military leaders, laying covetous plans for military conquests that ordinary people had to fight. At least in today's world, most modern war leaders do not claim to have God's ear or his help in planning strategy. Public education has eliminated that ploy.

Keep in mind that prior to the biblical stories, and for long afterward, human history consisted of armies surging back and forth over the area adjacent to the Mediterranean. In these wars, the victors enslaved the defeated. Dynasties rose and fell, and wealth moved back and forth between victors and losers. It is no compliment to the human race that, after engaging in wars for thousands of years, vast numbers of people do not yet realize that wars do not produce peace. The history of Israel is a good example of the rise and fall associated with conquest. After each defeat the objective was revenge, an emotion that religion finds acceptable even in the mythical deity; humans keep repeating the cycle as a result. The impact of religious stories on the mind, beginning with the young mind, blocks out inconsistency, such as simultaneously upholding peace while endorsing a scripture filled with war and the deviant behavior of its heroes. Strange? The power structure created a deity to fit human emotions, including aggressive behavior.

Like everything else, time has also changed the art of war. Primitive humans finally recognized that the cost of maintaining an army exceeded the value of the loot. The population increased, attracting to cities thousands of people who then formed governments that also adopted aggressive measures. The military role was transferred from individual leaders to large centers and countries. Even in biblical times an army had to be staffed and financed. The scope of the biblical wars raises questions of exaggeration by patriarchs. The story of Joseph and Mary has them journeying to report for census and to be taxed. Rome, the occupying power, needed men, weapons, huge quantities of supplies, and staging areas. No doubt an invading army probably lived partially off the land. Do you suppose the peasants in biblical times were compensated for the crops and livestock that armies may have commandeered? Would the poor, struggling peasants dare to protest?

The census, as noted in the Bible, was needed by the controlling power structure as a source of manpower for war. As cruel as these battles were, one incentive for joining may have been self-preservation. If your tribe was about to be invaded, your choices were few. From the biblical stories, wars were almost constant, and the average person had little choice but to join. Now, a few thousand years later, does it appear that human behavior has changed a great deal? For decades the U.S. military budget has wavered between being the second or third highest expenditure in the federal budget. Do you care to venture a guess when the public will recognize that neither war nor faith in a mythical deity will bring peace?

As noted, the cost of conducting war finally outstripped the value of plunder, even after the sale of captured slaves that Judaism and its mythical deity endorsed. Military power in the hands of governments then evolved into colonialism, enhancing national egos and giving the right to plunder natural resources in foreign lands. As national military changes took place, Christianity's power structure kept pace, often colluding with national governments, with the excuse of saving the souls of pagans in the New World. Take, for example, the sixteenth-century foray of Spain and Portugal into Central and South America during the reign of King Ferdinand and Queen Isabella. This invasion decimated an estimated one-third of the native population of Brazil. By the late seventeenth century, Spain had also crushed the Mayan civilization, like the U.S. mischief in Vietnam, where killing villagers was considered saving them. A moral question: How does Christianity justify the slavery and abuse imposed on natives, particularly in Central and South America? No evidence shows that the invading nations and the colluding religion ever offered to compensate the invaded countries for the brutality inflicted or the resources stolen.

The divisive nature of religion is actually the cause of many wars. Hate generated by religious differences is as violent as it gets. Consider the terrorism in Ireland, Afghanistan, the Sudan, Yugoslavia, India, Indonesia, and Nigeria, to name just a few venues. Reason is not compatible with faith. How can a reasonable mind justify the destruction caused by war in Yugoslavia or Afghanistan or the thirty-year war in Europe between 1616 and 1648? In the century just completed, more than one hundred wars killed over one hundred million people. Europe sacrificed forty-five million lives in World War II alone. Twenty-two million crosses stand for unknown soldiers in French cemeteries Do you recall God ever trying to stop or mediate these horrors? The errors in this seeming conundrum have a long history devoid of logic, reason, and certainly education. Where has God been? Why were prayers not answered? A more difficult question is why have humans not recognized they have put their faith in a myth? The time has come for logic and reason to look at the real nature of the universe and the psychological characteristics of the human species.

One reason for the slow uptake by humans is that many people find science does not provide quick and easy satisfaction. Myths seem to give quick answers. Also, science keeps changing with each new discovery. This can be unsettling to a person lacking a basic background in science, particularly one in whom religion has already instilled fear. Another hang-up may be that although science discovered the physical laws of the universe, it does not promise immortality as religious myths do. Myths of immortality appease the ego. Though science has lifted humans to healthier and longer lives, religious dogma does not require logical thinking. Science has determined that Earth is billions of years old, not something less than six thousand years, as determined by the Bible's genealogy. Through science and archaeology we now know that humans have been on this planet for millions of years, rather than the short time described in the biblical story.

IRRECONCILABLE MYTHS

❧

In Exodus 33:20 the Lord tells Moses, ". . . No man shall see me and live." Scary isn't it, after religion tells us that God is a loving father? The Bible has many inconsistencies. Read on and you are told that Moses and others saw the Lord face to face. Religion is adept at disguising its inconsistencies. For example, after every catastrophe, such as the destruction of the World Trade Center Towers in New York on September 11, 2001, believers hurry to beg for God's blessings. No cleric or believer dares to be so blunt as to ask the question: Where was God during all the months and the years that this despicable act was being planned? Similarly, it would be impolite, maybe even blasphemous, to ask God why he did not alert someone, at least the CIA and FBI, a few minutes before the terrorists struck. Even IRA terrorists in Ireland frequently warn someone in England that a bomb had been set. The problem is that in every calamity, whether the Oklahoma City bombing, a mudslide that buries thousands of humans, an earthquake, or a hurricane, the allegedly loving God gives no prior word of warning. Humans had to discover through science and some hard knocks ways to detect signals of pending catastrophes.

> **Is God Willing to Prevent Evil but Not Able?**
> *Then he is not omnipotent.*
> **Is he able but not willing?**
> *Then he is malevolent.*
> **Is he both willing and able?**
> *Then whence cometh evil?*
> **Is he neither able nor willing?**
> *Then why call him God?*
> —*Epicurius, a Greek Philosopher (341–270 B.C.)*

Had the logic of Epicurius been followed, the world would have become safer long ago.

How easy it is to deceive. It is understandable that a naïve nomad living in biblical times with no knowledge of the world could be taken in by the fear and myths promoted by a power structure. But today, in what are considered developed nations, it is difficult to understand the absence of reason and, therefore, the continued belief in myths. Failure to read the Bible, coupled with the willingness to believe the fear proclaimed by clerics, gives control to the perpetual power structure of the Judeo-Christian outlook on religion. Another reason that many people support religion is the fear of ridicule by the masses, particularly when one is unprepared to defend an individual belief. For example, history indicates that most people have always longed for peace, but history documents that religion does not produce peace; rather it creates the divisiveness that causes unending wars. Has the common person been misled by religion's power structure? Check the Old Testament; its stories frequently describe war as killing everything, and implementing a scorched-earth policy. Human progress is extremely slow because humans had to start with a blank sheet and evolve, learning everything on their own. The mythical deity left nothing but commands, the work of a power structure that used its authority to eliminate doubters by stoning them to death.

Without a written language, something the mythical deity forgot, human progress was almost nonexistent for millennia. The invention of a written language is credited to the Mesopotamians, beginning with a cuneiform style about 3800 B.C. It is estimated that some biblical stories appeared in written form around 600 B.C. However, millions of people are still illiterate today. It is hard to believe that a loving deity gives a hoot when so many people have always lived miserable lives. Their advancement depends entirely on compassionate humans willing to help them out of the mire. In so many cases, though, the lack of education and honesty in government leadership in these desperate localities makes short-term relief efforts almost useless.

Although many people are turned off when they detect favoritism, it is frequently expressed in the Bible. The myth has God picking favorites. Is this a contradiction? Because favoritism is in the Bible, it is accepted that God grants enormous favors to Abraham, without even mentioning how Abraham's qualifications exceed those of others. All we are told is that Abraham is the foundation for Israelites to claim to be God's chosen, a claim that is repeated over and over. No historical data exists, except that God liked Abraham, like in modern politics. The story, and it is only a story of a typical patriarchal legend, glosses over murder, stealth, robbery, and a tribal power structure, justifying invasions and plunder. The deity in the story serves as a ruse, a flimflam to control ignorant nomads. If this story were to start today, it would not be an easy sell. Though no proof of the ancient story exists, which makes it only hearsay, many people continue to believe it. All that is required for belief is to be told by clerics dressed in fancy regalia that favoritism is approved by the Bible, though the Bible is a document filled with dishonest and immoral acts.

Seldom are any questions asked about the Lord's generosity in promising Abraham in Genesis 13:14–15, "All the land thou see, to thee I will give it, and to thy seed forever." Nothing is said about what happened to the people that Abraham uprooted or what these people did to turn this deity against them. The story is clearly a cover for stealth and robbery by faking a dialogue with a mythical deity. Give religion's power structure credit. The story justifies stealing from others, and believers do not fault it even today. The biblical story has the Lord saying he will make Abraham ". . . the father of a multitude of nations." This obscure statement is of course hearsay, but three religions claim Abraham as their direct connection to God. The big three are Judaism, Christianity, and Islam. Judaism even upgrades its claim by declaring that God chose the Hebrews and their descendants as his chosen people. Throughout history this egotistical claim has cost the Jews many, many lives. Only hearsay supports Judaism's claim, but then hearsay is the foundation of all religion.

Only a minimum acquaintance with the Bible is required to detect God's pattern or modus operandi. It is immediately apparent that God deals only with one person at a time, a warrior or warlord. These select warriors enforce their privileged position by threatening death to anyone questioning the omnipotence of the deity with whom they are having private conversations. The concept of democracy and freedom of information had to be invented by humans after many years of biblical secrecy, oppression, and abuse practiced by both church and state. We know from history that our civil society was not initiated or promoted by religion's secret institutions. Fortunately, most humans have more favorable social attitudes than exhibited in the Bible and have even provided laws in recent decades that prohibit the threats and abuses found in the Bible. Government officials are now required to conduct open meetings, and this advance for freedom was secured by hard-won battles with monopolistic government attitudes and without the help of religion.

MONOTHEISM

The logic and reason that developed monotheism came from early Greek societies and was also known to exist at an early date in India and other Asian societies. These early leaders concluded that monotheism was a more reasonable approach than a whole basketful of mythical deities. Monotheism had gained popularity long before the ignorant tribes of Israel copied it as part of their legends and religion. By the time the ancient legends and tales of Israelite patriarchs had put it in writing, the influence of Asian thought had filtered into emerging religions. The patriarchs developed the story of Abraham coveting land and kept it alive for centuries. However, public relations and promotions had not been invented. Hence, the deity's message was amateurish, providing no facts or proof. Even by the time of the New Testament, principals in stories like those about Jesus could not write, requiring stories to be produced decades later by authors alleging to be reporting the leading character's message.

Stop to think about these stories. Why would an all-knowing and all-powerful deity, wanting to get a message to humanity, make no prior announcement of the main character's arrival, provide no coverage during the main character's life, then allow established cults and religions to collude with the occupying government to eliminate the main character in a manner reserved for thieves and criminals?

In ancient and modern times, political and religious power structures in particular, direct attention away from their inabilities to resolve domestic problems by diverting attention to foreign or remote forays. The ancients used a messiah to resolve problems. When the New Testament stories were written, Jesus was a focal point for blaming both church and state for the oppression and poverty of the masses. Zealots of this nature do not last long, even today, but Jesus' bravery was rewarded by the belief that he was the long-awaited Messiah.

ABRAHAM AS A MODEL

Taking a closer look at the alleged beginning of the three major religions, it will save time to skip the creation myth in Genesis. It is worth touching briefly on the genealogy in Genesis 11 because it lists people who lived for hundreds of years. You can do that in fairy tales and myths. Would you believe that one named Shem lived five hundred years? Keep in mind that many believers maintain the Bible contains no errors, as it was written by the divinely inspired. Of course, if there were no errors in the biblical story, we would be living on a flat Earth; check Revelations 7:1 ". . . four angels standing on the four corners of the Earth, holding up four winds of the Earth." This assertion also appears in Isaiah 11:12. Or consider this bit of horticulture from 1 Corinthians 15:36: ". . . and seeds would have to die before they can sprout." Unfortunately, the all-knowing, loving creator provided no nutritional data that would extend our life span. Humans had to develop their own science for answers to nutrition and health. Nor did the mythical deity mention diseases, germs, or viruses that need to be included in the creation theory.

Though the Lord took a liking to Abraham in the early part of the Bible, the story paints Abraham as a person who takes all he can get. This impressed the Lord, and he tells Abraham, "In thee shall all families of the earth be blessed." A rather broad statement, but let's move on to Genesis 12:7, when Abraham is in Canaan. The Lord appears and promises a fertile valley to Abraham, omitting any rights of people already living in Canaan. If the Lord did not covet, certainly Abraham did, and the story does not mention Abraham being excused from the commandment on coveting. In Genesis 15:18 the Lord is even more generous and promises Abraham the land extending from the river of Egypt (the Nile) "unto the Euphrates River." Now that is a chunk of land, encompassing the land lying between Egypt and land constituting Turkey, Jordan, Syria, Iraq, and Saudi Arabia. Tough luck for all the people already living there; they were not the Lord's favorites and apparently were on another list. As the saying goes, if you are looking for sympathy, you can find it in the dictionary, but since dictionaries did not exist, it was just tough luck if you were not a favorite of the loving deity.

Though this legend is the foundation of three religions, a little thought and logic makes it nothing short of a cover for greed and delusions of power. No doubt, Abraham intended to conquer the land described, and the legend provided the cover. If you read further into the Scriptures, you will learn that Abraham turns out to be a liar and a panderer with a bunch of concubines (interesting qualifications for the father of the three major religions), but he is the Lord's favorite. When Abraham arrived in Canaan he found it suffering from a famine that somehow the Lord failed to pass along to his favorite warrior. So Abraham moves on to Egypt where he passes off his wife

Sarai to the pharaoh, declaring Sarai to be his sister. No problem with this; the Bible even tells how to sell your daughter. Is it possible the Lord acted as a double agent at times? The parties to this drama interpret plagues that occurred naturally in Egypt as punishment for this spurious sale of illicit sex. The Pharaoh in this story was a bit more moral than Abraham and became suspicious that Sarai was not Abraham's sister. The pharaoh sends both Abraham and Sarai packing. However, the story reports that by this time Abraham was rich in livestock, silver, and gold. The moral: crime does really pay.

Later in the story, Sarai, who is barren, agrees that Abraham needs an heir and agrees to let Abraham impregnate her maid. (Immaculate conception was not yet in vogue!) Then problems arise between Sarai and the maid. For some unexplained reason, the Lord decides to change Sarai's name to Sarah, maybe to get her mind off the pregnant maid. We also learn that Abraham and Sarah are both more than ninety years old. Does it seem a bit strange that the Lord had not arranged for Sarah to be pregnant long before this, at least before Abraham got the maid pregnant?

This biblical story was developed and enhanced for centuries by patriarchs, who kept the Lord conferring with Abraham. To keep pulling the scam and ensure a continuing cult, Abraham had to guarantee the Lord that all males would be circumcised. Does this seem a strange requirement for starting a religion? Well, it is all part of the historical myth. Circumcision was widely practiced for years in more developed areas before the Israelites adopted it as part of their religion. The easiest way to enforce a rule among ignorant tribal people was to declare it as a command of the Lord. However, if the Lord was the creator of all that we see, and he sensed a defect in his design of the penis, why couldn't the alleged all-powerful Lord redesign the penis and save the pain and butchery, particularly since the Lord had not told anyone about anesthesia? As for anesthesia, humans had to develop it along with all the other medical and chemical knowledge that the all-knowing deity in the Bible did not even mention.

History and archaeology tell us that at the time of the biblical stories the most advanced civilizations were in India and Asia Minor. Overland trade by camel caravan made regular contacts between Mediterranean cities and Asian populations. Does it seem logical that a deity wanting to inform humans of his existence and looking for ways to send a message to his progeny would pick the most backward, superstitious warriors of Israel to promote his message of peace and justice? It is more likely that the power structure of Israel's tribes borrowed bits of religious dogma from their contacts with caravans moving east and west en route to Mediterranean cities. What we have is a story concocted by Israelite patriarchs, a story to serve as an opiate to control the ignorant masses. When legends were ultimately put into writing and later assembled into what is known as the Bible, the errors, contradictions, and endorsements of wars were all included. Though the stories are old, a vein of commercialism exists—namely, enriching a select few in the power structure at the expense of many.

HISTORY REPEATS ITSELF

A similarly callous attitude toward acquiring land by force exists today as the crux of the Israeli-Palestinian dispute. Israel's claim to land is based on its ancient religious myth of being God's chosen people and an equally mythical claim of being promised Jerusalem as a homeland for Jews. Why would such an important matter be a secret transferred by a deity to only one person, a warrior who claimed to be on speaking terms with the deity, supported only by a myth? The mythical God sure lacked foresight. His alleged wisdom had no concept of the violence that would result from promising one group the land that was occupied by others. His compassion for mankind also takes a hit for ignoring justice and compensation to those forcibly removed from their land to make room for his favorites, the Israelites. If you read the Bible, you could easily conclude that God likes conflict and killing. What do you expect when the Muslim Palestinians, other members of the alleged troika in the Abraham story, believe Jerusalem is also a holy place of Islam? Each has as much proof as the other, as both stories depend upon hearsay. Give credit to religion for another war.

ISLAM'S CLAIM

The Qur'an, or Koran, is the Muslim equivalent of the Bible and was written around the seventh century. Abraham, an adherent of the religious troika believed all prophets were human. Abraham, Moses, and Jesus were elected by God to convey God's religion. Muhammad was the greatest and was a direct descendant of Abraham. Could the divinely inspired writers of these stories have gotten the wrong message? But read on. The Muslim prophet Muhammad is alleged to be the divine remedy for distortions caused by mere prophets—namely, Moses and Jesus. Does competition in religion help? With all these loose ends the door was open for competing power structures. Islam reduced Jesus, considered to be God's son, to the role of a mere prophet, and the top deity did not even whimper. Perhaps Abraham's claim of being the source or foundation of three religions was considered so ancient, or far removed, that name calling by a sibling was trivial. Of course, if you examine the story closely, an Achilles heel remained that the top deity missed in spite of his alleged wisdom. The conflicting claims within the troika, or the three religions, opened a chasm that allows each religion to claim to be God's chosen. This made a perfect setting for the continuous bloodletting that occurred and which continues to this day.

The conflicts in Ireland, India, Indonesia, Sudan, Nigeria, and the so-called Holy Land are a few examples of the divisive nature of religion. For a comparable situation to the Holy Land, try to imagine religious beliefs in the United States that deny certain sects from entering a church or parcel of ground, because some flat-Earth era mentality declares the spot to be sacred. Here in the United States we are fortunate that scores of nationalities live together without this religious conflict, at least at present. Credit the separation of church and state in our Constitution for this benefit, though some conservative religions currently attack this safeguard. If victorious, the effect will be to introduce new conflicts. The fanaticism associated with sacred sites and promises of a homeland made by some myth is reminiscent of Adolf Hitler's mistaken belief in a master race— a distorted belief of skewed nationalism that resulted in horrific violence. Most humans, regardless of race or religion, are capable of living in various parts of the world among other nationalities and of becoming citizens of their host country. Many countries allow freedom of religion or belief in no religion. Fortunately, developed countries, at least those not closely resembling a theocracy, do not have the problems of ancient myths regarding sacred sites. Only religion engenders the deceit, hate, and aggression necessary to restrict and limit entry to an alleged sacred site or building.

The founding fathers of the United States had the foresight to provide for the separation of church and state in the U.S. Constitution. However, over a period of several decades our national government, along with some U.S. citizens, have contributed large sums of money and military equipment to Israel. This action involves the United States in the Mideast conflict.

This action also resulted in unintended circumstances that no one wants or dares to correct. The Israeli lobby in the United States and the special interests of military equipment contractors now exert pressure and influence on members of Congress to continue U.S. support to Israel. The chances of the United States being an impartial mediator in the Mideast conflict are therefore nearly nil.

AFRAID TO ACT

～o～

Humans who glue themselves to the status quo ensure that existing power structures will continue. The chance of exploring alternatives and new ideas is impeded or lost. One of the lost opportunities in history is the failure to recognize lessons that could be learned from years of persecution of Jews. To begin, it is a mistake to define or construe a religious belief as a nationality. The genes of residents of Middle Eastern people are thoroughly mixed from centuries as nomads and from wars and intermarriage. The people are similar, except for religion, environment, and education. The missed opportunity is the failure to recognize that persecution initiates a drive to survive, often by acquiring knowledge and specializing. A survivor is likely to think of being a citizen of the world rather than a specific nationality. The lesson to be learned is the demonstrated strength of character and achievements that accrue to individuals who become free from nationalism. Nations already recognize the benefits gained from talented residents. Of course, overcoming entrenched nationalism takes time, but accepting the concept of a category of world citizenship could provide an incentive for greater service and achievement regardless of where talented people reside.

RIGHTS VS. RESPONSIBILITIES

~~o~~

Conflicts, either local or at the world level, could be reduced if individuals accepted responsibility for their actions. This is particularly important in dealing with procreation, as the population explosion is affecting many nations. Because legislators are primarily interested in reelection, they are unwilling to challenge archaic Judeo-Christian myth to be fruitful and populate the earth. If a basic tenet of government is equity, transferring the cost of supporting the entire population to society is a violation of the equity principle. Because legislators lack the courage to uphold equity by requiring a person to be responsible for their actions, legislators divert attention by redistributing the public's personal income. Husbandry that includes a careful management of resources needs to be applied to more than plants and livestock.

Overpopulation in nature results in many plants and animals dying for lack of space and nutrients. The biblical position on procreation is also that of nature, and as humans we view this as brutal, hence our efforts to neuter pets. Because humans claim to be the superior species with the mental capacity to think and plan ahead, it should be obvious that the basic problem of most nations is overpopulation. The biblical myth served warlords who needed an abundance of grunts for their wars. In addition, unrestricted procreation was a male thing because the Bible considered women as chattel. Today tens of thousands of young people flee their homelands in search of employment, hoping to find a better life. Every facet of daily life—including education, employment, social services, the economy, and crime—is affected by the dilemmas that the biblical myth has created. A major obstacle to even bringing this dilemma before public consideration is religion's domination of state and federal legislators. Religion, of course, thrives on poverty and ignorance.

Coping in One World

⁓o⁓

In 1940 Franklin Roosevelt won a third term for president of the United States; his Republican opponent was Wendell Wilkie. Both candidates for the presidency were enlightened people and were thinking of the future. Wilkie's domestic program did not differ greatly from Roosevelt except for policies affecting business. In 1942 President Roosevelt appointed Wilkie to visit several nations to observe and gather thoughts regarding a postwar world. It is not known whether Wilkie coined the term "One World," but it was used in his report and he wrote a book in 1943 with that title.

The concept of one world that one should have in mind involves improving the general welfare without jeopardizing freedom. The one world proposed more than a half-century ago was not ready for the concept of world citizenship referred to above. Though overlooked to date, it needs to be considered as a fresh viewpoint to counter the continuation of dead-end, obsolete nationalism and foreign policy. Today technology adds to the one-world concept by increasing the talents and knowledge that could serve well to enhance many deprived areas. In addition, the experience of the oppressed may offer information about resolving conflicts in battered parts of the world. World peace needs a better alternative than the continuing wars caused by religion's ancient mythical beliefs.

THE DAMAGE CAUSED BY LEGENDS

∽∘∾

The story of Moses is a major legend in the biblical story. Legends serve to reinforce belief and offer role models, though the biblical legends portray criminals when viewed by standards of modern society. Throughout the ages myths had similar patterns even though the locations were far removed. A typical ancient myth involved an abandoned child who is miraculously saved and in later life becomes a great leader. Perseus, the son of Zeus, slays Medusa, a Gorgon woman who is always pictured with snakes in her hair. Perseus then marries Andromeda. The Romans invented the legend of Romulus and Remus, the story of twin brothers who were abandoned and then raised by a female wolf. As adults these two brothers are credited with founding the city of Rome. The legend of Moses is strikingly similar to a Babylonian legend that existed centuries before Moses. By coincidence the Israelites were at one time captured and enslaved by the Babylonians. Do you think this period of slavery in Babylon might have influenced the story of Moses?

The story of Moses mimics the Babylonian story of a noble woman who apparently wanted to escape the shame of having an illegitimate son. She places her baby in a boat made of reeds and lets the boat drift down the Euphrates River. Then, just as in the Moses legend, the babe is rescued and raised as the son of the rescuer. No proof exists for any of the legends. However, in a period with no media for communicating over long distances, orally transferred stories could be used almost anywhere without the knowledge of the source. Because the ability to put anything into writing came long after the biblical story, people always had ample time and opportunity to enlarge or even change the story while being orally passed along. After the invention of writing, the ancient spin doctors were the patriarchs with a vested interests in maintaining a power structure.

Like all biblical stories claiming to be guided by God, the Moses legend provides nothing about Moses' early life. The story jumps from a babe in a basket to an adult in Egypt. In Exodus 2:12, Moses performs one of his first recorded acts, which happens to be criminal. However, criminal acts are common in the Bible. The biblical description of the criminal act committed by Moses is as follows: ". . . looking this way and that way and seeing no one, he killed the Egyptian and hid him in the sand." Moses had to escape and the story has him going to Midian in the Arabian Desert, across the Red Sea. Historians divide the biblical story of Moses into segments. One time interval is from his birth to his escape from the crime in Egypt, a period estimated at about forty years. The next interval begins in Midian where he is herding sheep on his father-in-law's property. Time passes until Exodus 4:19, when the Lord tells Moses, "Go, return into Egypt for all the men are dead that sought thy life." We have the Lord protecting a murderer until it's safe to do another job for the Lord. Let's face it, if your life's work includes aggressive acts, you need help from time to time, and having an accommodating God in the story sure helps sustain and build the power structure.

Being a successful storyteller meant competing with many existing myths. The Roman and Greek myths of Hercules and Zeus provided a number of early mythical stories. Though interesting, the story of Moses has a certain problem; it cannot be verified, nor is it mentioned in any other historical documents. This is strange, because Egyptian history is considered quite detailed, and makes no mention of the Moses story, including the mass exodus of Israelites serving as slaves in Egypt. No evidence of the biblical story remains on Egyptian temple walls, tomb inscriptions, or fragments of papyrus. Actually, the biblical story conflicts with historical facts, because at the time of the Moses story, around 1300 B.C., Egypt was occupying the northern Sinai coast, the area of Canaan, extending as far north as the Euphrates in Syria. Egypt's army developed forts at the distance of a day's travel. Archaeological studies have unearthed remnants of these fortifications. These facts raise numerous questions on the credibility of the biblical story of Moses.

Another undocumented story of the Bible is of Moses and six hundred thousand Israelites escaping from Egypt and continuing to wander in the desert for forty years. No archaeological evidence has been unearthed that would verify the story of this vast number of people, the equivalent of a large city leaving Egypt, roaming the desert for forty years. It stretches the credibility of the Bible's divinely inspired writers. This tale also raises doubts about whether the story of the Mosaic Law and the Ten Commandments really took place during this period. Like all warring nations, Egypt finally exhausted itself in conquests along the Sinai and the Mediterranean coast. A final battle with the Philistines in Canaan forced Egypt to withdraw exhausted. The Philistines too were greatly weakened, which may have allowed the Israelites at a later date to enter and occupy Canaan, as mentioned. Note that the Bible story of Israel's invasion of Canaan includes God as a coconspirator in planning the invasion.

An interesting conversation occurs in Exodus 24:4 between the Lord and Moses, which established the rights of slave owners. A slave master gained the rights to a slave's wife and children. If a slave decided to continue with a master, the master had permission to bore a hole in the slave's ear with an awl. Today that act would represent branding, and though the allegedly compassionate God participated in this plan, it would be ruled as cruel and inhuman treatment by courts of developed nations. However, the Bible approves of numerous acts that today would be considered cruel and inhuman punishments. A few years ago residents of a school district in Louisiana removed the name Jefferson from their school because residents of the school district objected to Thomas Jefferson having been a slave owner. Nothing was said about the school district residents destroying their Bibles, though the Bible endorses slavery. Of course, humans are not required to be either consistent or logical. The action of the Louisiana school district says something about how little people know about the Bible, though many claim it to be their moral guide.

To date the current Mideast violence in the area called the Holy Land has not been compared with Exodus 23:23–24, where the Lord offers His angels to lead Israel's army to cut down the Amorites, Hittites, Perizzites, and Canaanites. However, the Lord also warned the Israelis not to bow down to the gods of the defenders, but instead he advises them to "utterly overthrow them." In addition, the Israelites are told that the Lord will, ". . . send fear before thee and will destroy all the people to whom thou shall come." With the Bible as a guide, peace is not to be near."

History Repeats Again

❦

For those who read the Bible, it probably seems that the Lord's message in Exodus 24:30 is being repeated. The Lord tells the Israelites: "Little by little I will drive them out from before thee." Though the Exodus account took place thousands of years ago, today's Mideast conflict is similar. Do two wrongs make a right? Claiming God promised them a homeland, the Israelis have been slowly taking land from the Palestinians without compensation. Another unexplained contradiction is in Exodus 24:9 where Moses and his close associate "saw the God of Israel." If that is the case, do other people then have a different god than the biblical one reserved for the Jews?

Over the course of history, Christianity—and in recent years, the U.S. government—have committed serious violations of the rights of believers of Islam. These accumulated offenses could have contributed to the attacks of September 11, 2001. For many years the U.S. government granted billions of dollars to Israel, along with valuable military information, while ignoring Palestinian objections to the taking of Palestinian land. The

U.S. government and other members of the United Nations have ignored Israeli violations of UN resolutions. Over the years few members of Congress have had the courage to question U.S. policies toward the Mideast conflict, because the few members of Congress who did speak out were not re-elected. To understand the Israeli power structure, read former Congressman Paul Findley's book, *They Dared to Speak Out*.

Is Ignorance Bliss?

❦

Judaism and Christianity are fortunate that very few people read the Bible. If a person applied even a bit of reason when reading Exodus, they would recognize the illogical, conflicting statements of the religious power structure that instills fear in the ignorant, superstitious masses. In Exodus 20:4–6 the Lord, who we have been told is a loving deity, admits to being jealous and claims that he will impose a curse on anyone who worships another deity, a curse that will extend into the third and fourth generation of the offender's children. That resembles voodoo and amounts to punishing the innocent. A deity that issues threats to competition is not on very sound footing. A dictatorial attitude and threats are expressed throughout the Bible and are a dead giveaway that the myth cannot withstand examination. For thousands of years this was the attitude of religion's power structure. Religion changed only after the public gained knowledge, forcing Christianity to abandon such violence as burning people at the stake during the Spanish Inquisition. The Taliban in Afghanistan and Reverend Jones's Peoples Temple in Guyana, South America, are modern examples of religious oppression.

SECRECY VS. TRUTH

⌘

The secrecy employed to protect the biblical myth continues in Exodus 24:12. Here the Lord asks Moses to come up on the mountain, saying, "I will give thee three tablets of stone and a law of commandments which I have written." Note the Lord issues only commands; nothing is ever offered to improve living conditions or to educate. Moses treats the invitation as a secret and threatens his subjects with death if they venture up the mountain. Moses then spends forty days and nights on the mount. The Lord tells Moses to ask his followers for offerings. Surprise? The power structure has never been reluctant to ask for money; ornate structures are proof of religion's success in extracting money. If you doubt these claims, read Exodus 25:26–30, where Moses springs an elaborate wish list on his followers. Of course, Moses was a sharpie; he tells his followers that all of this was the idea of the Lord, who they were not allowed to see. Believers forget that Jesus is not quoted as asking for posh, ornate buildings, though the Old Testament is not bashful about garnering wealth in any manner possible. Tithing is mentioned right from the start of religion's story. In Genesis 14:20, Abraham claims to have given part of his loot to God, though we don't know just how that was done. Tithing, or giving 10 percent of your income, is mentioned in Genesis 28:22, Numbers 18:21, and again in Deuteronomy 12:5–18. For centuries parishioners have struggled to meet the financial requests of their power structures, though most parishioners live modest lives or in poverty.

MOSES THE SCHEMER

The trip Moses made up the mountain for a secret meeting with the Lord cost the followers a bundle. Moses told his followers that the Lord asked for gold trinkets and carving for the sanctuary, a gold-covered table, gold-plated dishes, gold candlesticks, curtains of linen, vessels with olive oil for burning, garments and offices for priests, onyx stones with the names of the leaders engraved in gold, golden chains woven in wreaths, and a gold plate engraved with the words "Holiness of the Lord" to be placed on blue lace. Sounds like the modern equivalent of furnishing the CEO office of Enron or WorldCom. It would seem that some followers of Moses would have recognized Moses was using this myth to satisfy his own ego. After spending forty years roaming the desert with Moses, the rank and file of believers have something to work for, in the hope their efforts will be rewarded in heaven, though no one seems to know just where that is (Neh. 9: 6, Ps 57).

Believers never seem concerned with biblical contradictions. In Exodus 33:20 the Lord tells Moses, "No man will see me alive." However in Exodus 24:1, "Moses, Aaron, Nadab, Abihu, and seventy elders of Israel come up unto the Lord." In Exodus 24:2 only Moses is to come near the Lord, then in Exodus 24:10 the full contingent is named again: "They saw the God of Israel." Distinctly, this says the deity belongs to Israel! This may be confusing until you recognize it is a legend handed down orally for centuries by Israelite patriarchs; it is their story. Not to be left out, non-Israelites later made up their own deity in the New Testament. Spin doctors scored a hit as they made up stories about Jesus, who became a martyr after being eliminated by the political intrigue of the established religion of the Israelites and the government of Rome.

Power Grows in a Vacuum

In Exodus 22 the people following Moses became impatient while waiting forty days for Moses to come down from the Mount. Sensing an opportunity, one member of the waiting group, Aaron, stirs up the masses and gets them to donate all their gold, consisting of earrings and trinkets. Aaron then melts the gold and forms a golden calf to be worshiped as a new god. Does it seem strange that desert wanderers who had been slaves in Egypt had this amount of gold? This fact is needed to add excitement to the story and emphasize the danger of accepting a competing deity. After forming the golden calf, Aaron builds an altar and proclaims a feast. Like a good mystery story, the Lord got wind of the deviant acts taking place and sent Moses down to check it out. The Lord's antenna must have worked better then; he didn't get even a whiff of what was going on for months, possibly years, by Al-Qaeda as they planned the destruction of the World Trade Center. Nor did the Lord sense anything while the bombing of the Murrah Federal Building in Oklahoma City was being planned.

Moses came down from the mountain carrying two stone tablets on which God had written on both sides just by using his finger. Moses, who must have been tired after carrying these stones, saw his people celebrating a new god. In anger Moses breaks the stone tablets. One would think some archaeologist would have found pieces of these stone tablets and either auctioned them or given them to some museum. As with all myths, though, nothing has ever been found, even in all the desert area where Moses and his followers allegedly spent forty years. Moses was determined to punish his deviant followers for the sin of worshiping another god, clearly an act of blasphemy that the Bible punishes with the death penalty. The teaching about loving your enemy apparently has limits (Lev. 19:18). According to the story, Moses throws the golden calf in the fire, then grinds it into a powder, tosses the powder into water, and forces the celebrating people to drink it. What drama! This has similarities to the Jonestown colony in Guyana, South America, where the Reverend Jim Jones founded the Peoples Temple. In 1978 a congressional delegation flew to Guyana to investigate possible human rights violations. In fear of retribution, members of the colony took or were forced to take poison. Over nine hundred people died in that incident.

Are the facts about Moses' reaction logical? What did Moses have in mind when he threw the golden calf into the fire? Is a wood fire hot enough to melt gold? If the gold was melted, it would have to be cooled again before it could be ground into powder. What did Moses have available to grind gold into powder? If he did get the gold ground to powder and put the gold dust in water, the gold would not dissolve. Forcing the people to drink the granular gold and water would be a bit gritty to swallow yet would cause no health problem. Not much thought was given to the details of this story, for clearly it is a fairy tale. The only purpose of this incident in the story was to show power and induce fear. The next episode in this story illustrates biblical revenge.

After Moses' temper tantrum, he asks for recruits—volunteers willing to support the Lord. We do not know how many volunteered, only that Moses instructs the volunteers to go throughout the camp slaying every man, his brother, his companion, and neighbor. The Bible says, ". . . About three thousand were killed that day." That slaughter by comparison downgrades the Jonestown massacre into a minor event. Moses was lucky; at that time in history no laws were violated, other than the commandments. Maybe Moses received special dispensation from the Lord, or maybe Moses had not had time to read the commandments he just brought down from the Mount. The story does not mention that the Lord objected to this or any other mayhem in the Bible. The mystery is how people today accept these violent myths yet still believe that religion will bring "peace on earth, good will to men." The ease with which myths can mislead the mind raises real questions regarding the intellect of the human species. Of course, very few people read the Bible, and going along with the herd is just easier.

Another war-and-peace biblical contradiction appears in Exodus 33–34 where God assures Moses that an angel will precede him as he drives out the Canaanites, the Hittites, Perizzites, Hivites, and Jebusites. The only reason given for this violence is that the Lord does not like these people because they pray to a different god. (The Taliban in Afghanistan didn't make that mistake; they carried the Qur'an into battle, and the deity never reprimanded them either.) If from early life one is told that the Bible provides a model to follow, then many will not recognize that the intent of Moses and others was to conquer, to steal the land belonging to Canaanites and others, using the myth of religion to justify their immoral and illegal acts. The Bible is a collection of stories invented by patriarchs to control backward, nomadic Israelite tribes and to justify the pillage and murder by warlords.

Getting back to the murders Moses carried out, the Bible says the Lord instructed Moses to destroy the altars and images of the tribes he invaded in Canaan and to increase the misery and havoc for the victims by destroying all fruit groves. The Lord liked scorched-earth tactics and recommend it as he planned invasions with his warlords. Somehow many people believe this, though it is a ruse, a lie that warlords used to justify their violent actions. This is cleverly covered by the Lord warning Moses and other warlords not to make friends or agreements with the people they drove out. All were excuses to justify plunder and murder. "Thou shalt not avenge . . . nor bear grudge, . . . but love thy neighbor," (Lev. 19:18) is really just stage dressing, a cliché used with tongue in cheek. The Lord warns of "whoring with the gods of the enemy." The myth of the Lord clearly fears those who apply reason, hence the use of death threats. Religion's strength lies in its adherents' ignorance of Scripture, for a thinking people would recognize the stories as a charade, a pretense, a ruse to justify aggression and to rob others of their property.

USING THE LORD TO ACQUIRE LAND

∾o∾

Exodus 34:24 explains the plan that is repeated by modern Zionism. The Lord, in this myth, directs Moses to drive out all tribes, declaring, "For I will cast out the nations before thee, and enlarge thy borders; neither shall any man desire thy land. . . ." This is the deity Christianity would have people worship, the deity that instructs Moses to invade Canaan, promising, "And I will send hornets before thee which will drive out the Hivite, the Canaanite, and the Hittite. . . . Little by little I will drive them out from before thee, until thou be increased, and inherit the land" (Exod. 23:28–30). The Lord then tells Moses, in Deuteronomy 20:12-17, how to deal with the victims: "Thou shall smite every male with the sword. But the women, children, cattle, and all that is in the city, . . . [t]he spoils thereof, thou shall take for thyself . . . but the cities, thou shall save nothing that breatheth. Thou shall utterly destroy them; namely, the Hittites, the Amorites, the Canaanites, the Perizzites, the Hivites, and the Jebusites, as the Lord hath commanded thee." Does this resemble the current Israeli-Palestinian conflict in the so-called Holy Land? The power structure of modern-day Israel denounces any who question its motives as anti-Semites, a smear tactic for diverting attention and reason through name calling, as perfected by Senator Joseph McCarthy in the 1950s when he smeared every opponent by calling them a communist.

What trust should one put in a God that selects as his chosen people a backward, primitive group, engaged in continuous war, plunder, slavery, and deviant behavior? Far more advanced civilizations existed at the time of the biblical stories. The secrecy involved on the part of the alleged deity—speaking with just one aggressive, scheming, Israelite warrior—should set off bells in most minds. Compare the Lord's action to a modern father who speaks secretly to only one of his several children, declaring the one child to be the father's favorite. Following the Lord, this reclusive father does not relate his prejudice to all the siblings, but allows the alleged favorite to inform the other siblings that he or she is Dad's favorite. Add to that the threat of death if any sibling doubts or refuses to obey the words of their father regarding his alleged favorite child. That is the Bible story reduced to the family level. Of course, the example would create a continuous battle within the family, exactly as religion has done to the human race. Using myths, murder, wars, Inquisitions, and secrecy, the power structure maintains control.

Moses Climbs the Mountain Again

❧

To complete the story of Moses at the mountain, the Lord tells Moses to bring two more stone slabs to replace the ones Moses broke in a temper tantrum, and the Lord agrees to write on the new stones. Nothing is said about Moses and his volunteer hitmen who killed some three thousand of the followers waiting at the foot of the mountain. The authors of this story should be credited for their wild imaginations. Too bad the broken stone slabs have not been found; Judaism and Christianity would have at least one item that could be proven. Instead they have to rely totally on hearsay and myths. Of course, no messages concocted by any religion, whether on stones or gold plates, have ever been found. Just out of curiosity, what language might the Lord have used when writing on the slabs, since all other biblical stories were orally transferred for centuries until writing was invented?

After Moses lugs two more stone tablets up Mount Sinai and presents them to the Lord, he stays another forty days and forty nights without eating or drinking. Today we know that anyone on a hunger strike for forty days is not in very good shape, but fairy stories are not bound by logic. The Lord writes the Ten Commandments again, but this time the story does not mention that the Lord wrote in stone with his finger. Might the Lord have employed fusion or fission to write on stone? If so, why didn't he pass that technology along to save humans the time in developing atomic power, along with the atomic bomb since the Lord enjoys war. The story doesn't mention Moses having a problem carrying this second set of stones down the mountain, though he didn't eat or drink for forty days. The Lord should have advised extreme care, so his work could continue to be on display, rather than limiting it to a story for Moses and his tribe.

The patriarchs should be credited for creating and maintaining some interesting stories, though the stories have the validity of Snow White and the Seven Dwarfs, or King Arthur and the Round Table. Quite likely the reason many people do not question the biblical fairy tales is that they do not actually read the Bible. The few people that have read the Bible were probably warned early in life of severe penalties if they questioned these ancient war stories. When fear is instilled early in life, the effect is like an indelible imprint on the human brain that serves as a flashback if doubt should occur. Early indoctrination implants an effective mental block to logic and reason.

The exaggerated story of Moses also credits him as the author of the Pentateuch, which is the title given to the first five books of the Old Testament (based on the Greek word for the number five). However, this credit to Moses is discounted today by most authorities on religion. That Moses lived 120 years should raise doubts as to whether the story is on a par with a Walt Disney production. Where would Moses find time to write five books of the Bible after spending years in Egypt, then forty years roaming around in the Arabian desert, followed by years of war and plunder as directed by the Lord? It also seems unlikely he could write about his own death, burial, and eulogy. The divinely inspired authors got carried away here. Would Moses have left a vague description of his burial site? Deuteronomy 34:6 says he was buried "in a valley in land of Moab"—that's all. The eulogy to Moses in Deuteronomy 34:10, "whom the Lord knew face to face," adds to the previous contradictions regarding the danger of seeing the Lord.

AFTER MOSES

The Book of Joshua would have you believe that Joshua was also hand-picked by the Lord to continue the invasion and conquest of Canaan that Moses did not complete before he died. However, archaeological evidence and scrolls that have been discovered raise questions about this story. The physical evidence gathered by archaeologists shows the occupation of Canaan occurred slowly, probably over hundreds of years, and most likely by infiltrating as the Canaanite populations declined. The area of Canaan was in the path of many wars fought over a long period of time by Egyptian and Philistine armies. Climactic changes could also have played a part in the decline of the Canaanite population. Archaeological evidence combined with studies by historians and biblical scholars conclude that the Israelites probably took over Canaanite cities and villages after these sites were destroyed by fire associated with conquests by other powers.

No archaeological evidence shows that the Canaanites built walled cities, which puts into question the biblical stories of

Israel conquering walled cities. The story of an Israelite army marching around the walled city of Jericho and destroying the walls by blowing their trumpets is fiction. Canaan was under the control of both Egypt and Assyria at different periods, the control shifting occasionally to one or the other over hundreds of years. It does not appear that Canaanites resisted either occupation; the people just happened to live in a territory desired by major powers. The final destruction in Canaan occurred as Egypt and Syria fought over the territory.

Because no communications systems existed in this era, it took years for stories to reach isolated areas. Historians conclude that patriarchs of the ruling power structure expanded or exaggerated the legends for effect and to impress listeners. Numerous excavations in these biblical areas have raised serious doubts about biblical accounts, including Joshua's massacre of the city of Ai. The biblical story describes the battle of Ai as a power play by Israelites. Applying just a bit of reason, it is unlikely that a band of unskilled, escaped slaves from Egypt, having roamed the desert forty years with Moses, could suddenly be prepared for a military takeover and an administration capable of decimating Canaan. Logic as well as archaeological evidence indicates that the Israelites acquired land by becoming squatters, and slowly over a long period of time becoming the dominant group. More than likely, conflicts occurred as the number of squatters increased and competed for resources, possibly similar to the current conflict between Israel and Palestine.

As archaeologists and historians study various excavation levels, analyzing implements, pottery, and remains of the Israelites, the evidence based on buildings, home furnishings, and ceramic ware do not compare with the Canaanite culture or lifestyle. The Israelites are judged to have lived at a lower-level lifestyle. Israel's initial settlements were located in upper elevations, on hillsides. The Canaanite villages were in fertile valleys. Evidence of public buildings, storehouses, temples, palaces, and luxury items were not found on Israelite sites. Though biblical stories describe continuous warfare, no fortifications or weapon relics have been found on the sites of the early Israelites in Canaan. A realistic conclusion is that the Israelites had difficulty sustaining life on the stony ground they selected or were permitted to live on. Olive groves and vineyards existing on the highlands where Israelite settlements were located indicate that the Israelis had a subsistence type of living.

Archaeological discoveries also contradict the biblical story of Joshua, which claims that Israel's army invaded and utterly destroyed Canaan, even describing some bloody battles. Again the patriarchs appear to have created their own history. In Judges 3:31, Shamgar slays six hundred Philistines with an ox goad. The wife of Heber slays the Canaanite general Sisera by driving a stake into his head while he slept. Does this violence of God's chosen people convince you that the Judeo-Christian God will bring peace? People who believe that the Bible is a family book should check out Judges 20:22–29, the story of a man offering his daughter and a concubine to a group of men "to use as they see fit." After a night of gang rape the concubine is dead. Her body is then cut into twelve pieces and distributed around the Israel's twelve tribes. It is important to note the Bible considers women the main offender of fornication, and distributing the concubine's body parts was meant to leave a message. Somehow, reading the Bible leaves the impression that God likes blood and mayhem, which is perhaps why so few people read it.

People who today committed the crimes mentioned in the book of Joshua, with God as the coconspirator, would be tried before an international court for crimes against humanity. Consider Joshua 8:24: "When Israel had finished slaughtering all the inhabitants of Ai in the open wilderness where they pursued them until the very last had fallen by the sword, all Israel returned to Ai and smote it with a sword." Add to these atrocities Joshua 8:25: "And all who fell that day, both men and women, were twelve thousand, all the people of Ai. Also check Joshua 8:29: "And he hanged the king of Ai on a tree until evening, and at the going down of the sun Joshua commanded and they took the body down from the tree and cast it at the entrance of the gate to the city. . . ." Nowhere does it mention what evil or offense the Canaanites or residents of Ai committed, except that they had different beliefs. Of course, that is all that is necessary for most wars today. However, one can guess that the story of Joshua was fabricated to impress listeners of the deity's power and, of course, to whitewash the criminal acts of the power structure. Archaeology has determined that the story is fiction, but it is alarmingly reminiscent of Adolf Hitler invading Czechoslovakia and other parts of Europe, with the excuse of gaining "lebenraum" (living room). It appears the biblical stories amount to the patriarchs designing history as they desired it and also to strengthen the role of the power structure.

Piecing a Picture Together

꙳

The origin of the current Israeli/Palestinian and other Mideast conflicts can be traced back to World War I. At that time the foreign secretary to Prime Minister Lloyd George of England was Arthur J. Balfour, who made known Zionism's interest in a homeland. The map of the world was about to change. Territory of the defeated Ottoman Empire, which included Palestine and historic Canaan, was to be divided by the Versailles Peace Conference, a body sanctioned by the League of Nations. A review of the work of that conference should remind current generations of the error of arbitrarily drawing national lines without allowing input from the people affected by those crucial decisions. Recall, for instance, Yugoslavia, the scene of recent violent ethnic wars. The initial partitioning of Yugoslavia was the work of the Versailles Peace Conference, and ethnic preferences were ignored.

At the close of World War I, England was still recognized as a powerful colonizing empire and for that reason was called upon to supervise a protectorate mandate over Palestine.

England accepted reluctantly. The mandate that England was to administer included what is referred to as the Balfour Declaration, permitting the Zionist movement to establish a Jewish homeland. This amounts to a national government giving preference to a religious group without consulting others who might be affected. The current efforts to establish peace in the Israeli-Palestinian conflict have not taken the Balfour Declaration into consideration.

Included in the Balfour Declaration is this statement: "It being clearly understood that nothing shall be done which may prejudice the civil and religious rights of existing non-Jewish communities in Palestine, or the rights and political status enjoyed by Jews in any other country." The Balfour Declaration overruled Arab interests when it accepted objections that Jews made on allowing Arabs to express their opinion. The excuse given by Jewish representatives was the Arabs would not establish a democracy. A U.S. group, the King-Crane Commission, was sent to Palestine to solicit Arab input and reported that the Arabs wanted the United States to administer the mandate while the Zionists wanted England to perform that function. Unfortunately, U.S. President Woodrow Wilson never saw the report as he was ill and had ceased to function as president. David Ben-Gurion is reported to have said, "We want the country to be ours, but we must wait for the great powers to decide at the Versailles Peace Treaty."

Britain soon became annoyed by the conflicts between Arabs and Jews and appointed Herbert Samuel, a Jew, to serve as an administrator of the mandate. Segregation became a problem; Jews demanded that street names be in Hebrew, even in exclusively Arab areas. The Jews called Palestine Erizt Israel, or "Land of Israel" and believed the British administrator to be anti-Semitic because English policy was to defer and allow time to negotiate and resolve problems. The Balfour Declaration came under pressure for redefinition, in particular the immigration policy and the ability of the economy to absorb the increased number of immigrants. The Jews began to circumvent the British administration and applied pressure directly on Britain's Parliament, as well as on the United States. By 1937 a national Arab movement had formed, and frequent demonstrations and clashes began to occur. In 1936 Ben-Gurion told Lord Peel, the British commissioner, that the Bible was the Jewish people's mandate.

The idea to divide Palestine between Arabs and Jews came under consideration, but very few seemed in favor. Ben-Gurion agreed to a division, provided that the plan transferred the Arabs. England would not agree to deporting Arabs, which caused a rebellion and forced England to move twenty-five thousand troops to Palestine. While World War II was in progress, Menachem Begin was leader of a militant group called Etzel. Years later Begin became prime minister of Israel and subsequently was awarded the Nobel Peace Prize. Another Israeli group formed during the World War II period was the Haganah, which was charged with stealing hundreds of rifles and one hundred thousand rounds of ammunition from the British army. Begin also enlarged on Ben-Gurion's reference to the Bible as the Jewish people's mandate, repeating the biblical claim to land extending "from the Nile to the Euphrates," a statement made by Abraham.

In August 1944 the Etzel group tried to assassinate British Commissioner Mac Michael. Military groups or gangs then operating in the Jewish territory were the Haganah, the Irgun, and the Stern Gang. In November 1944 an opposition group murdered Lord Moyne, a senior British representative located in Egypt. Anti-British terrorism grew to a campaign in the Jewish community. In 1946 the Etzell gang blew up the King David Hotel used by the British, killing more than ninety people. Another incident was the mining of streets leading to a British commissioner's formal dinner party. The mines were discovered, but the dinner was canceled. With one hundred thousand soldiers committed to Palestine and two Britons killed every day, Great Britain turned the mandate of Palestine over to the United Nations. In November 1947 the UN voted to divide Palestine into two states, one Jewish and one Arab; Jerusalem was to remain under international control. However, the proposed border was so long and circuitous that it posed a very difficult task for control and seemed to set the stage for war.

What conclusions can one draw after analyzing the big picture of history? It amounts to a few dominant, warriorlike, scheming individuals who constitute a power structure, using a mythical god to control not only the ignorant and superstitious masses, but national governments as well. Following myths was not prudent in ancient times, and the divisive intent of religious myths continues to threaten the lives of many today. Still some fear to question the mythical story of a loving, all-powerful deity, though that deity spoke only with warriors, making the message only hearsay.

Given that the Israelis represent less than 1 percent of world population, is the other 99 percent of the world condemned, or do they need a separate god? Nowhere in the mythical stories of the Bible does it ever explain what this deity has against the other 99 percent of the world population. Of course the story was a ruse, a cover for plunder and stealing land. Neither the Judaic religion nor any other religion has challenged the Bible's genealogical calculations that determine the age of the world at less than six thousand years. It does not take a nuclear scientist to observe Earth's geological deposits that along with the discoveries of astronomy have provided the evidence that the biblical story of creation is a myth that satisfied ignorant nomads.

With the Bible alleged to be a guide for humans it is no wonder that throughout history humans have continued to murder, plunder, rape, and enslave each other. To accept a mythical god, who in the stories is a bloodthirsty, covetous, and devious character, is no compliment to human intellect. It is even more bewildering to find so many people willing to accept Israel's mythical claim to a "promised land." Today many Jews no longer practice or support that ancient faith and assimilate into society wherever they choose to live. They are no longer beholden to the divisive, inflammatory dogma that restricts association with other beliefs or defines who can be accepted as a Jew. It is erroneous to consider the word "Jew" as a nationality; it is a religion. Indoctrination can produce side effects, and the Jewish religion is no exception. Adhering to ancient tribal rules has made Jews a target for persecution. Of course there is a flip side to the coin; persecution stimulates resistance and determination to survive, to become an achiever. This trait also appears today among Asian immigrants. It is hard to believe that among educated people a religious fanaticism that restricts entry into sacred buildings or sites can still exist on the basis of an ancient myth.

An example of the divisive characteristics of religion is the competing claim to a site deemed sacred to Jesus and Muslims. Temple Mount to Jews is the Noble Sanctuary to Muslims. In September of 2000, in the presence of hundreds of police and military personnel, Ariel Sharon entered the disputed site, rekindling the Intifada and the fall of the Barak government in Israel. Was Sharon's act deliberate? To consider oneself a chosen people based upon an ancient myth devised by a covetous, aggressive power structure is not likely to be well accepted in most societies. Such a stance is an invitation for abuse, for it smacks of self-judged superiority.

Unfortunately for world peace, the Israeli power structure has adopted the policy of declaring every difference of opinion as anti-Semitic. After receiving the world's sympathy for the terror and sacrifices imposed by a despot during World War II, it now appears to many that the oppressed have become the oppressor. The remorse felt for the Jewish victims in World War II tends to obliterate the huge sacrifices made by others. In World War II Russia lost more than three times more people than the Jews. War is hell, and yet a vast number of people consider the Old Testament guide holy, when it is really a collection of stories invented by a power structure to camouflage violence, to steal the wealth of others, and to enslave captured victims.

The military mind has difficulty understanding a basic law of physics: the law that for every action there is an equal and opposite reaction. That law applies to social conduct as well. The most effective course for humans to reduce an inherent human tendency toward aggression will come through education. Unfortunately, budgeting for education is often treated like a poor country cousin compared to military expenditures. If indeed there was a loving, all-powerful deity, why did his earthly lieutenants, the clerics, oppose education for centuries? The number of humans killed in wars in the twentieth century alone exceeds 100 million, and from all indications the twenty-first century will keep the pace. If imploring some deity for peace for thousands of years has not brought results, is it not time to alter the direction of the search?

SEARCHING FOR ANSWERS

∽∘∾

In the centuries between the time depicted in the Old and the New Testaments, a few inquiring minds appeared among people living along the Mediterranean coast. Aristotle, Socrates, Plato, and Pythagoras, to name just a few, began to analyze, compare, and apply what is known as reason to make deductions. It is hard to imagine the deficit in knowledge, the ignorance that existed in the early years of the human race. The few observant individuals who dared to think drew the conclusion that the basic elements were water, fire, earth, and air. Such a degree of ignorance should give pause to the biblical myth about creation. How can one believe in a loving deity that would leave its progeny in complete ignorance? Of course, the earth looked flat, but for a power structure that claimed to be on speaking terms with the Lord, the myth leaves much to be desired.

As noted above, a few early Greek thinkers began to examine the world, to apply reason, and to make deductions. In time some early thinkers formulated the bases for mathematics and philosophy. Some of their conclusions continue in use today. However, the early thinkers met resistance from fellow humans. Socrates tried the patience of many; he had the reputation of questioning others, asking them to explain or defend their beliefs. This ticked people off. Therefore, the leaders, the power structure of the day, declared Socrates a threat to young minds and sentenced him to death. Socrates was forced to drink hemlock, which killed him (it was the best remedy they had except for stones!. For a time the prevailing ignorance was protected from progressive ideas. Dinosaur-like leaders fail to recognize that it is hard to kill ideas. Thoughts can be suppressed but not erased. A residual effect can and did exist for centuries, eventually bringing the Age of Enlightenment. No one remembers Socrates' oppressors, but Socrates is still known.

The growth and development of the Greek civilization expanded, benefiting the entire Mediterranean area. Greek education enhanced political and commercial activity. Aristotle, a student of Plato, was a member of Greek government and taught Alexander the Great. The Greek empire at one time extended over much of eastern Mediterranean and into Asia Minor, influencing government, architecture, education, and commerce. Greek culture may have been the moderating influence that changed the style of thinking and writing, resulting in less emphasis on wars and killing in the New Testament. The New Testament stories were written in Greek and Aramaic and later had to be translated.

What a difference exists between the writing style of the Old and the New Testaments. The Old is a contrived story of a warmongering deity, who colluded with warlords, coveted the land of others, and raised no objection to the theft, rape, incest, and slavery carried out by his top lieutenants. At the time of the New Testament the social contacts and development favored Greek civilization. Writers of New Testament stories considered it necessary to portray a caring deity rather than the wars and exploits of the abusive power structure that dominates the Old Testament. This transformation took a long time, but public opinion tires of violence. Most human wants to be left alone and to conduct their lives without coercion and threats by either government or religion.

Of course the power structure that selected the books that compose the New Testament kept the myth of God, even though this allegedly loving, all-powerful deity had not passed along one bit of knowledge about life and the universe. A myth cannot be greater than the minds that create it. In those early days, and to some extent today, not a clue existed to explain the purpose of humans or any other life form on planet Earth. Besides, it was easier to continue the myth, because humans seemed to enjoy an array or a choice of myths that served to fill the black hole of ignorance. Myths eliminate the embarrassment of not knowing. However, today it takes only a small amount of time to know enough science to be comfortable with being a part of an exciting, mathematically exacting, and continually expanding universe. It is a cop-out to believe the biblical myth about creation, of life created from a bit of dirt, in contrast to recognizing that humans and other life-forms consist of RNA, DNA, neurons, and so much more. It is even worse to accept the servile, scullion-like, secondary role that the creation story allots to women.

In developed nations new information continues to expand on the subjects of biology and chemistry. It would be a lazy mind that did not have some knowledge of the human body and other creatures. The inquiring mind is fascinated by the challenge of understanding protons, neutrons, molecules, DNA, proteins, and the transmission of electrical impulses. Whether or not we completely understand our role in this vast universe, educated people find pleasure and satisfaction in productive lives and in being a participant and contributor to this exciting, ongoing world. Of course if one does not feel whole or safe without myths of heaven, hell, and the flat Earth, they should be free to hold those beliefs. However, this does not give them the right to demand that everyone else believe the same thing. The intolerance humans have toward different beliefs and races produces conflict.

As far back as we have been able to reach in history, aided by archaeology, paleontology, carbon dating, and other sciences, evidence shows that regardless of where early groups of humans lived they created cults or religion to fill the vacuum, the black hole of human ignorance. Without the aid of education, basic animal instincts prevailed, including forming power structures that used force, conformity, and killing to maintain control. Myths provide an ideal foundation for power structures. Because either proving or disproving a myth is difficult, the power structure rules by commands, often including the right to kill dissenters. Each mythical religion had a creation story, and quite often the power structure claimed the mythical deity had to be humored or pacified with sacrifices, often using humans. Those in power recognized that fear is the ultimate means of control. Some credit can be given to beliefs, even false ones, for they may offer some feeling of security. However, facts and information are the best long-term solution to insecurity. None of the power structures or their deities provided the knowledge to enhance life, cure illness, or reduce a life of drudgery.

History indicates that the early Greek, Roman, and Egyptian religions and cults were quite tolerant of each other. They did not claim to be exclusive or consider the gods of other people to be devils. The early Roman religion had no priesthood. Those serving the role of priests were civilians, and their sermons did not threaten others with damnation or claim "this is the truth" and compel someone to believe and support it. It took the Christian, Muslim, and other organized religions to use armies to force acceptance of their beliefs. Intolerance for other beliefs became the norm. Though the differences are usually small, competing power structures are at stake, and violence enters to settle the matter. Violence committed by believers has ranged from terrorist acts on each other to partisan wars to the burning of opponents at the stake. It is ironic that a story claiming to represent kindness and love is instead filled with violent acts that continue to this day.

PERPETUATING FEAR

∽o∽

The educational system in developed nations should be concerned with the violence and threats in biblical stories and recognize that they were employed in ancient times when ignorance and superstition prevailed. Fear and commands were basic weapons, though defeating in the long run. The learning process should avoid superficial, quick answers offered by myths, and instead erase areas of fear with steps that determine cause and effect. For instance, what causes ongoing poverty in so many parts of the world? Not a beginning subject, of course, but the education process should seek to develop solutions. What problems have been solved by myths?

Humans seem to be drawn to myths, superstition, cults, and religion to offset insecurity. Humans as well as other species do not handle insecurity well. This weakness or characteristic can be observed in small children, as they adopt objects to serve as security blankets. It is not uncommon for children to create imaginary people or creatures and treat their make-believe object as a steady companion. Aesop's fables appeared around the sixth century B.C. and were considered a valued addition to child development. These fables did not attempt to use fear, but instead made long-lasting mental imprints through morals and pleasant associations. Adults also respond to stories for the purpose of reducing or relieving insecurity. Charismatic leaders recognize the fear induced by insecurity, and by claiming clairvoyance with a deity, they can clinch loyalty and support. A person looking for a quick fix can be hooked by the central theme of Bible stories, which is to "accept commands and be obedient and you will be saved." Check out Deuteronomy 13:3: "...for the Lord your God proveth you, to know whether you love your God with all your heart and all your soul." If you have doubts or are inclined to raise questions about the autocratic, totalitarian, or oppressive system demanded by the Bible, then Deuteronomy 13:10 will get your attention: "[T]hine hand shall be the first upon him to put him to death, thou shall stone him until he die."

The Bible mentions some early practices of ancient governments that have not changed—namely, census taking and tax collection. Joseph and Mary in the biblical story are fulfilling this duty in traveling to Bethlehem. Even in those early days governments conscripted soldiers and seized the public's wealth to support wars. Some things just don't change. We know from history that the lives of early, primitive people were bleak, oppressive, and frequently brutal. They had good reason to aspire to a vision, to accept a prophecy of relief in an ethereal, visionary world. Except for a few developed nations, a large number of people on Earth still continue this visionary search for relief from violence, pestilence, and injustice by believing in some imaginary place. The poor in undeveloped countries are apt subjects for a promise of relief from their misery. A promise is at least a ray of hope. When people have little chance for education they soon recognize that they cannot escape from a dead-end existence. Confronted with such an existence people are easy picking for the cunning, the crafty, and the skilled shaman to take control.

A contemporary book on the World War II era, *Hitler's Pope* by John Cornwell, implicates Catholicism as participating in the power structure that dominates a repetitious scenario of war. Eugenio Pacelli, Pope Pius XII, who was considered by the Vatican as an agent of God, was the first to diplomatically recognize Hitler's Third Reich and never withdrew that recognition. The Vatican was also silent when the Italian army invaded Ethiopia in October 1935 and Albania in 1937. The Vatican praised Franco during Spain's civil war in the 1930s, during which half a million lives were lost. In April 1939 Catholic churches in Germany said prayers for Hitler's fiftieth birthday. God does not appear to have ever stopped humans from carrying out wars, murders, terrorism, and endless kinds of corruption. How could a myth take any action? The nature and acts of humans create problems. Just adding another myth, the devil, to take the blame for the inaction of the mythical God did not change anything.

In his book *Decline and Fall of the Roman Empire,* Edward Gibbon labels the Crusades organized by the Vatican to kill Muslim infidels as "human idiocy." Gibbon evaluates history in general as "little more than a register of the crimes, follies, and misfortunes of mankind." Most wars center on religious differences. Though much evidence is available to raise suspicions of complicity, religion has not yet been associated with the costly and humiliating Vietnam War and the flim-flam excuses as well as lies offered by the U.S. government to justify a military presence in Vietnam. It is hard to understand how U.S. citizens could be made to believe that the backward, relatively primitive country of Vietnam—with no air force, no navy, and located halfway around the world—could possibly be a threat to our security. Logic and reason are not strong traits of the human race.

Unfortunately, the public often allows governments to escape with less than the truth, using answers that cannot withstand close examination. This costly dereliction allowed Secretary of State Allen Dulles, formerly the CIA director, to sell the concept of the "domino theory," which circuitously served to involve the United States in Vietnam. The domino theory alleged that all backward parts of the world would fall to communism unless the United States intervened. Never mind that the economic and social problems that existed in undeveloped countries would inundate any country trying to take them under their wing. The only reasons Vietnam or any other poor and backward nation would accept communism would be their extreme poverty and lack of education. An impoverished people have little choice. Our so-called experts could not foresee this, apparently unable to understand that humans never put up with oppression indefinitely. Those factors were irrelevant; special interests hoped to benefit by involving the United States in Vietnam.

Our entry into Vietnam unfolds something like this. Shortly after the end of World War II the French army invaded Vietnam, intent on reestablishing what was part of their prior colonial empire. The French army misjudged their adversary and became encircled by the North Vietnam Communist army. The French army suddenly faced annihilation. For some reason the U.S. navy was already in Haiphong Harbor. The United States was asked to assist the French army, which was being pummeled by the North Vietnam Communist army. Initially the United States sent advisors to Vietnam on the premise of supplying only advice to the nondemocratic South Vietnamese government. When President Johnson and his secretary of defense faked a naval incident in the Tonkin Gulf, the special interests had their excuse to conduct a full-scale, albeit undeclared, war, which dragged on for years.

This unpopular war, to some an immoral act, killed some fifty-four thousand U.S. troops and ended in a humiliating defeat. During this war a split or schism developed in U.S. society, affecting morals, education levels, and a mistrust in the integrity of public officials that continues to this day. One can ask in hindsight: Should the president and his supporting staff who lied about the Gulf of Tonkin have been charged for war crimes before the International Criminal Court? Do we seem to hold a double standard when we approve of other national leaders being charged for war crimes but demand exemption for our own leaders and military personnel?

Morally the United States should have refused giving assistance to France in its effort to reestablish colonialism in Vietnam. A question that has not been explored is, was the U.S. entry into the Vietnam War related to the special interest of Catholicism, a dominant religion in Vietnam? Could religion have influenced President John Kennedy to send advisors to Vietnam, or Allen Dulles, our secretary of state, to conjure up the domino theory and sell it to a gullible public? This possibility has never been closely examined. Evidence indicates, though, that the United States was pushed into this quagmire.

God Ignores the Poor

❦

Religion continues to deplore poverty, but is unable to provide an answer to this perpetual problem due to religion's historic stance of opposing birth control. Although religion no longer opposes education, it does not approve of sex education that includes birth control, and is even able to control foreign aid that would provide prophylactics that could reduce the spread of AIDS. Religion's alternative to the excess of poor and uneducated people is to advocate public support, placing the burden on society. The human species appears to be alone in thinking that someone else should support them. Ample evidence throughout nature illustrates the pain and death resulting from unlimited procreation, but the biblical myth blinds humans from reason, logic, and the responsibility for feeding, educating, and housing the children they produce.

The Bible's reference to poverty even seems flippant, remarking only, "The poor will always be with us." Has the allegedly all-knowing, all-powerful God admitted defeat and just written off the poor? Religion also recognizes that its greatest strength is with the poor and the uneducated. Poverty and a low education level provide a fertile field for religion. Hence, Catholicism and other conservative religions oppose birth control and family planning, and they remain silent on the problem of violence at birth control clinics.

This barbaric stance influences state and federal legislators, who pander to any organized group. The damage is felt worldwide, for Congress refuses to address overpopulation in undeveloped countries, where poverty and ignorance feeds world terrorism. Instead of applying aid to this human problem, the U.S. government offers military supplies and mob and riot control training. Because world problems now spill over onto U.S. soil, our legislators are busy increasing home security legislation that erodes personal freedom. In addition to ignoring poverty and lack of education as contributing to terrorism, our government supports corrupt foreign governments, supplying them with military equipment and training their armies and police forces.

Religions allege they support peace, though historically the major religions used military force to achieve their dominant role. People used force to introduce religion into all of Europe with the exception of Ireland, which initially escaped invasions because it was too remotely located at the time. However, Ireland has made up for lost time with its religious violence for the past four or five decades. Islam also employed armies to impose its belief system upon people, beginning about the sixth century and spreading over much of northern Africa and into Asia. Christianity's esteemed St. Augustine justified war on the basis that men had always fought and therefore it had a place in Christian behavior. It was not difficult then for St. Augustine to add that war could be waged, provided it was done by the command of God, thus making for "just" wars. Myths need a lot of support, and again, if you do not know history you are condemned to repeat it. The next step in religion's doctored logic was to approve of wars claimed to be by divine command to convert the heathen and destroy the heretic, which was the Vatican's cover story in launching the Crusades. Of course the Old Testament provided the example; the word "slaughter" was frequently used to described wars in which the mythical God co-conspired. Religious myths unfortunately continue to justify territory expansion and claims in the so-called Holy Land. Finding a war that religion ever objected to would be difficult indeed.

THE NEW TESTAMENT

The Christian religion began as a cult, and required several hundred years before it was considered a religion. Though Christianity claims Jesus as its advisor and teacher, he wrote nothing; the biblical stories were written years after Jesus' death by persons not acquainted with him. Religion carefully avoids that Jesus is never quoted as favoring a new religion, even though some stretch the myth to make him the son of God. As noted before, Jesus' message was that of a reformer, condemning the oppressors, consisting of the dominant religions and the Roman government. Why would Jesus have given thought to a new religion, when he was convinced that judgment day was near, as predicted in the Old Testament? Mark 13:30 is one of several references in which Jesus is alleged to have said, "Verily I say, this generation shall not pass until all these things be done." Well, Jesus was not the first to err in judging this call, even if he was the son of God.

From history, archaeology, and other sciences we know that advanced civilizations existed, even in the Andean and Central

American regions, at the time God is alleged to have selected the primitive, ignorant Israelites as his chosen people. For Jesus to be quoted as saying the end was near tells you something about the backward people who originated new religious myths. At the time of the New Testament, thriving business and commerce centers and education systems existed in population centers around the Mediterranean Sea. However, Christianity and Judaism would have us believe a backward tribe of warring Israelite nomads was God's selection, worthy of carrying the deity's message of salvation to all mankind. What an indictment to human intelligence! Consider, also, that at the time of the biblical myth Greece was already a world power. Alexander the Great, a student of Aristotle, stopped the spread of the Persian empire in the fourth century B.C. and spread Greek architecture, language, and commerce into northern Africa and as far east as the Himalayas. In Egypt where the Nile meets the Mediterranean he founded the city of Alexandria. The city became an intellectual center, attracting scholars from Greece and as far away as the Orient. The followers of the new cult destroyed centers of learning introduced by the Greek civilization, including the library in Alexandria.

From about the third to the fifth centuries, the number of monks attracted to the new Christian cult came mostly from the lower social strata. Monasticism attracted misfits, criminals, homosexuals, fugitives, plus a few pious. It was a career for ignorant peasants, appearing at times as gangs to bully competing religious sects and civic groups. They were known to interfere with commerce, shipping, and business, comparable to a later era of the Mafia. It was not an auspicious, respectable start for religion, a history that religion does not care to discuss. To find more on this period, read *The Transcendental Temptation* by Paul Kurtz; *Asimov's Guide to the Bible* by Isaac Asimov, and *The Bible Unearthed* by Israel Finkelstein and Neil Asher Silberman.

The new cult that evolved into the Christian religion did not have a respectable start. The alleged loving deity who one would suppose had an interest in guiding the new religion appears to have abandoned it to opportunists who then established the power structure.

About 385 C.E. Christian bishops destroyed the libraries in Alexandria, a center that had become a collection of some seven centuries of classical literature, science, history, and philosophy. This is not surprising, because for centuries Christianity's hierarchy did not cotton to education. Myths do not fare well where education thrives. Alexandria had been an international center of learning and commerce, and the Greek language prevailed. As previously noted, Greek was the language of the educated, of commerce, and the New Testament Gospels over a span of decades. A few Gospels were written in Hebrew and Aramaic, requiring translation for the Greek-speaking audience. Egyptian Jews even had the Torah translated into the Greek language, referring to it as the Septuagint, meaning seventy, the number of days and men required to complete the translation.

When Alexander the Great returned from conquering parts of Asia Minor he contracted a fever and died in Babylon in 323 B.C. at the age of thirty-three. Alexander is recognized for making the first notable and lasting impact on a vast area of civilization. Why wouldn't a deity that wanted to attract wide attention, by preparing a scripture and teaching the ignorant masses, select a leader of Alexander's stature? The answer lies in the power structure of each religion and the commandments of fear that are required to maintain a story based on hearsay. In the real world Alexander was felled at the height of his career, apparently by malaria, a bacterium. If you believe in the creation story, the bacterium that killed Alexander was also part of the mythical deity's work, along with a countless number of diseases and natural disasters. The allegedly loving, all-knowing deity left not a single clue on combating disease, even to his favored Israelites.

ACCORDING TO THE STORY

❧〇❧

The biblical story of Jesus' activities took place in rural and exclusively Jewish regions. He moved among fishing towns and agriculture communities of Galilee, where dissent against Rome was common. Jesus returned to his hometown of Nazareth, and according to Matthew 13:55–56 he met an unfriendly crowd. The audience is quoted as saying: "Whence has this man this wisdom? Is not this the carpenter's son?" Jesus left Nazareth and did not return. Speaking in his home community, Jesus drew no comments regarding divine status, great destiny, or his virgin birth. Jesus' father Joseph is referred to as a carpenter and by inference Jesus is called a carpenter. Jesus may have been a laborer or a go-fer in modern job descriptions. Certainly his inability to write was a serious oversight for a person selected to transform the world. According to Matthew 13:55, Jesus had five brothers and several sisters, though Catholicism presents Mary as a lifelong virgin. But given that very few people read the Bible, almost any story is safe.

After Jesus' death, Peter became the nucleus for people attracted to Jesus' message. The sect or cult continued in a loose form, observing Jewish law and worshiping in the temple. As is true even today, humans tend to splinter into groups, and this occurred after Jesus' death. The vitality of the Roman empire at the time of the biblical story stimulated the growth of the commercial class and provided employment for the unskilled, the equivalent of slaves, which religion did not object to then or for almost two more millennia. Quite some time after Jesus' death, Saul, a Jew from Tarsus and a Roman citizen, came into the picture. He later changed his name to Paul. As a part of the commercial class Saul had contacts with the poor and the working class. He was also a declared Pharisee, rejecting at the beginning of the biblical story the belief that Jesus was a messiah.

The first mention of Saul in the Gospels is his participation in stoning to death a man named Stephen, a spokesman for the cult whose language was Greek. Stephen was considered a foreigner in the Judea and Galilee areas, a person with different ideas, name, and possibly religion. Stephen's declared crime was a speech he made, protesting oppression (similar to comments of Jesus), which is noted in the New Testament (Acts 7:56). Because Stephen protested oppression, he was charged with blasphemy that under Mosaic Law is punishable by death. Plenty of people seemed ready to support the power structure and employ the death penalty. No deity ever interfered. Stones were the weaponry of the time; it achieved the same end as a gun, but you had to enjoy brutality close up to participate.

As a Pharisee Saul made searches of churches and houses, imprisoning men and women who believed in cults, including the new cults that formed after Jesus' death (Acts 8:3). Saul's background posed no problem for the biblical story. He was in good company with other biblical heroes, who included murderers, seducers, slave merchants, and those who believed in treating women as chattel to be abused and kept silent. All the spin doctors had to do with Saul was arrange a transformation, which was done on a trip to Damascus where Saul has a seizure, is blinded, and hears the voice of Jesus. Saul's loss of vision lasts for three days, when mysteriously the curse was lifted by being touched by a member of the new cult living in Damascus. (Mysticism really enhances a story.) Saul was cleansed, he confessed his past that included murder, and he could now speak for the Lord. That he changed his name to Paul was convenient.

Analysts of the biblical story suspect that Paul was epileptic and that he had a seizure on his journey to Damascus, causing him to see burning bushes and hear voices. Epilepsy, like everything else in those days, was not understood, and his seizure was classified as divinely inspired action. Humans commonly assigned anything they did not understand as divine. Labeling the unknown as a miracle was not limited to uneducated ancients; it is often applied today. Modern analysts of the Saul/Paul story who believe he suffered from epilepsy note that other Scriptures describe Paul as rigid and unbending, characteristics associated with epilepsy. In one instance his behavior was such that he needed the protection of an entire regiment of the Roman army to escort him from Jerusalem to Caesarea. Second Corinthians 10:10 describes Paul as follows: "[H[is bodily presence is weak and his speech contemptible." It helps to understand that Paul grew up as a citizen of the Roman empire, that he was educated in Greek, and that as a Jew he followed the religion of the temple that opposed the increasing number of religious sects. Being educated in Greek, Paul would have been familiar with Plato's philosophy that holds goodness as a virtue with its own reward and righteousness as a human quality. This teaching could have caused Paul to question the brutality of crucifixion, requested by the religious power structure of that time. Paul is quoted in Romans 2:10 as saying, "Glory, honor and peace to every man that worketh good; to the *Jew first,* and also the Gentile" (emphasis added).

It is doubtful Paul ever saw Jesus, for if he had Paul would certainly have said so. It did not take long for the new cult to recognize a problem with admitting Gentiles. Jews opposed the new cult for they did not believe that Jesus was divine or that he fulfilled the role of the Messiah as forecast in the Old Testament. Certainly, the end forecast by Jesus did not occur—namely, that the Lord would soon appear and settle the injustice in the world. (Jesus, of course, was not the first nor the last to miss predicting the end of the world.) The Jewish opposition to and dissent regarding the new cult caused Paul and fellow believer Barnabas to move frequently. Initially the new cult followed the religion of the Jews in rejecting Gentiles, and Peter and Barnabas are said to have refused to eat with Gentiles.

BENDING THE RULES

If you are starting a new cult, you need supporters for clout and for gathering money in the collection plate. Paul, Peter, and Barnabas had to find a way to diplomatically admit Gentiles. Some fancy mental gymnastics would be required to exempt Gentiles from the Mosaic Law of circumcision. A major symbolic smoke screen would be required to paper over old beliefs, including the ban on eating with Gentiles. It should be noted that these disputes were about men, because women were not considered worthy or eligible, except possibly to bake cookies and feed the roaming missionaries. Even as late as the fourth century C.E., the Council of Laodicia decreed that women were excluded from the sanctuary, from approaching the altar, or even from touching sacred vessels. No one seemed in a hurry to change this, for as late as 1917 the Canon Law (Canon 813.1, Catholicism) prohibited women from approaching the altar, and any responses from women were to be made from a distance. Some of this legalism was inherited from pagan religions that Christianity absorbed. Medieval churches did not allow women behind the sanctuary, and choirs were all male—with sopranos supplied by castration. Talk about enlightenment! It took almost two thousand years for male domination in Christianity to begin to change, and some male dominance still continues. Some Baptists still adhere to the belief of submission of women.

Paul's missionary work and the promotion of a new cult probably benefited from the widespread objection to Roman rule and the yearning for a messiah predicted in the Old Testament. The geographic area of the eastern Mediterranean, known as the Fertile Crescent, had also benefited from the Greek civilization transplanted by Alexander the Great. Though the Roman Empire had gained control at the time of the biblical stories, Greek language and culture still continued over a wide area. Only small, isolated towns and rural areas like Galilee and Judea retained Jewish customs, and in these remote areas Jesus lived and worked. The Gospels do not indicate that Jesus was ever a part of the Mediterranean commercial development, making it possible to conclude that Jesus did not have the opportunity to be literate.

After Jesus' death the mix of apostles and other self-styled advocates began offering numerous versions of Jesus' message. Splinter groups formed among dissidents of the established, predominant religion of the Pharisees and Sadducees. However, the usual run of cults that existed within the Jewish population—and history records many—did not seem to threaten the dominant religion. As new cults began to emerge after Jesus' death, each with its own interpretation of Jesus' message, threats and resistance rose. Paul's background probably divided his loyalties for a time. His knowledge of Rome's use of crucifixion to humiliate and torture enemies may have persuaded Paul to consider and then accept what he was hearing about Jesus' message.

The rejection of the new cult by Jews meant that Paul was confronted with overcoming the Gentiles' objection to circumcision. Just like clever politicians today, Paul formed a committee to study the problem. True to form, the committee found a way for both sides to win. The politics of power structures do not change. To appease believers in upholding Mosaic Law, the committee recommended exemption from circumcision, provided the new inductee agreed to refrain from pork, to abstain from the pollution of false idols, to promise not to fornicate, to abstain also from things that had been strangled, and to promise not to consume blood. What a bunch of unrelated gobbledegook, but it was enough to circumvent the old custom of circumcision, dating back to Abraham in the Old Testament. Peter, the apostle who denied Jesus three times, came up with a real clincher. Peter announced that God spoke to him with a message for the Gentiles. The message was that God saw no difference between Gentiles and Jews when their hearts are purified with faith (Acts 15:9). However, this gives no indication that God altered his opinion of the Israelites being his favorites. Clearly, Peter demonstrated his qualifications as a superior politician. No wonder he is the rock alluded to in Christianity.

It seems a bit strange that God would have tired over the problem of founding a religion on circumcision and taken the opportunity to clear up the matter. Peter could also have helped by saying God spoke and admitted that his earlier discussion with Abraham that set the requirement of circumcision was a bit much. Had God been honest he would have admitted that the custom of circumcision was in use in developed and advanced societies at least two hundred years before He sold Abraham on the practice. However, the mythical God has never tried to avoid creating dissension and conflict among his children.

With just a little reason it would seem that someone would have to ask what makes circumcision so important when it is not visible whether a man conforms to this trim job or not? It would seem that a brand or mark on the forehead would have aided religion in separating believers from infidels. Wouldn't a loving, kind God just admit he made a mistake in designing the penis and issue a recall? If he is really the creator, why not correct the mistake with a miracle? An honest deity would have advised the Jews to leave circumcision to personal choice and not continue the practice as a part of religion. However, a still larger question needs to be asked. Why is this ancient practice still continued today when humans finally solved the problem of cleanliness? With no help from a deity the foreskin of the male penis can be rolled back for cleaning, thus making surgery on infant males unnecessary and a somewhat cruel act. Custom and tradition often thwarts knowledge.

Speaking of cruel acts, in 1 Samuel 18:25–27 King Saul required David to collect one hundred foreskins in lieu of a dowry for the king's daughter in marriage. The king thought David would be killed and the king would not have to put up with David as a son-in-law. The king misjudged David's' ability, or maybe David's fervor and affection for the king's daughter. David killed two hundred men, presented the king with the foreskins, and won the king's daughter. That warrants reading in a family circle. David is a hero in the Jewish religion. How? Like all biblical heroes, he made it to the top through war and conquest, the type of action admired by the mythical deity. David's reign was followed by his son Solomon, a family man described in 1 Kings 11:3 as having seven hundred wives and three hundred concubines. He built elaborate palaces, and like all religious leaders he used the money garnered from people who had a hard time making ends meet. Again, history and archaeology do not substantiate these stories. They are myths created by ancient patriarchs who exaggerated a lot and invented their own history. These stories do not appear in any other recorded history or coincide with archeological findings. The biblical stories are on a par with the tales of King Arthur and the Knights of the Round Table. Although biblical stories extol violence, war, and slavery and are sustained by myths comparable to voodooism, they served the power structures well by using the power to eliminate objectors.

Paul and Peter demonstrated political skill in maneuvering to exempt Gentiles from the Mosaic Law on circumcision without infringing on myths. Both men were astute enough to recognize the power of superstition, magic, demons, and spirits. Peter was adept in injecting the mythical deity's wording to allow non-Jews to escape the Mosaic Law. A more useful solution to this dilemma would have been for God to explain how to make soap and, even better, how to produce a potable, safe water supply. The Bible represents only a report on the history of the ebb and flow of the lives of a backward, nomadic people and how their destiny changed with their wins and losses. The patriarchs of the faith continued the myths, adding exaggerations to supply the need at the time.

CUSTOM AND TRADITION

∽o∽

In reading the Bible stories it is important to recognize that ages before the time of Jesus humans had invented festivals to celebrate death and resurrection. Inscriptions on inner walls of pyramids and tombs dating three thousand years before Jesus document these celebrations. In John 11:25 Jesus is quoted as saying, "I am the Resurrection and the Life," a phrase lifted from Egyptian chants in 700 B.C. by the Egyptian god Osiris, the judge of the dead. Remember, Jesus wrote nothing himself and what he is quoted as saying is largely the work of people who did not know him but definitely were guilty of plagiarism. After all, if you are writing to support a power structure and improve its finances, your story should be as interesting and as inspiring as all other stories in existence. We know from history that the major civilizations had arrived at monotheism long before Jesus was born. We know the miracles and morals attributed to Jesus are also found in the Old Testament and in some pagan religions. Stories of births, deaths, and resurrections used in the Bible were borrowed from pagan myths, rather than being divinely inspired. Likewise, Jesus' use of the golden rule in Luke 6:31 is a copy of advice used by Aristotle and Confucius, as well as in Hindu tradition.

Nowhere in Paul's efforts to start a new religion does he mention Jesus' birthplace, the virgin birth, the miracles, or the healing Jesus is alleged to have performed. Paul does mention several times that he too agreed with Jesus' belief that the end of the world—when the Lord would judge everyone—was near. That statement would instill fear, as was intended, and reinforce the illusion held by many that Jesus was the messiah predicted in the Old Testament. Magic, astrology, demons, and superstition prevailed and served as substitutes for knowledge. People in those early times drifted in and out of cults, even belonging to more than one at a time without serious problems. One myth was as good as another. In *The Rise and Fall of the Roman Empire,* Edward Gibbon describes the prevailing attitude in those early times as follows: "The various modes of worship which prevailed in the Roman world were all considered by the people as equally true; by the philosophers as equally false; and by the magistrates as equally useful."

In the developed world today many people would be in strong disagreement if they took time to read some of Paul's recommendations. Even though many minds are trained almost from birth to accept and not question biblical writings, they would take issue with such statements by Paul in 1 Corinthians 14:34: "Let your women keep silence in the church. And if they will learn anything let them ask their husbands at home, for it is a shame for women to speak in the church." Or 1 Timothy 2:12: "But I suffer not a woman to teach, not to usurp authority over the man, but to be in silence." Now, almost two thousand years later, we find the Taliban in Afghanistan imparting these same lessons, even though they are working out of a different scripture. Perhaps Paul's chauvinist attitude was responsible for the more modern expression, "Keep them bare-foot, pregnant, and tell them nothing!" Paul's ministry did not help women's lot in life one bit, nor did religion and the Bible object to slavery. This should come as no surprise for the Bible is a document written by men to establish a power structure, and to rationalize murder, genocide, and theft of the land and wealth of others. The role of women is that of chattel set by an elite, self-perpetuating hierarchy that unfortunately still exists in far too many parts of the world.

Not until recently have some religions rejected the biblical ranking of women as second class, relegating them to provide bake sales, to make and sell clothes, rugs, and bedspreads to augment the support of churches, the salaries of male ministers and staff, and to contribute financially to religious hierarchies and establishments that are now worth billions of dollars. Whenever church leaders decide to polish or enhance their social obligations by helping the poor, the fund raising often falls upon the women in the church. No thought is ever given to liquidating the gold and other embellished treasures the hierarchy has accumulated in national and international structures. No evidence shows that Jesus meant to create the royalty class and rank that exists in religion. Jesus' message clearly objected to power structures, not just to the oppressive Roman Empire, but also to the power of the Pharisees and Sadducees. Jesus' ministry, at least as it is reported, states people do not need intermediaries to address their God. Jesus believed people can address God directly. Of course, no established religion will concede that clerics are superfluous. Vast numbers of people are destined to continue what author George Santayana's observed: "Those who cannot remember the past are condemned to repeat it."

Finally in the twentieth century, a time lapse of almost two thousand years from the beginning of Christianity, only a few religions have extended equal rights to women. Notably absent in the list granting equal opportunity are Catholicism and Islam. As usual in human history, the early pioneers for women's rights such as Elizabeth Cady Stanton were often jeered and abused. Even the U.S. Constitution, an enlightened document in most respects, failed to acknowledge the equality of women and had to be amended in 1926 to grant this franchise. How could this have happened? You might say it was standard procedure for such a long period of time that it was overlooked. Even though the authors of our Constitution recognized the restrictions and oppression of freedom and human rights caused by religion in the Old World and had the insight and intelligence to require the separation of church and state for our new nation, the force of religion's sexual discrimination for at least two millennia made this oversight automatic.

The Catholic hierarchy grants sainthood to some women, an honor now being considered for Mother Teresa. What is noteworthy of her service? Through her work some of India's indigent received cover, a cot, and food. What lasting effect did her work have on class, human relations, India's economy, or the reduction of the number of destitute people? Sex education and the distribution of condoms would have had a greater impact on what is a major problem in developing nations. Of course, religion's greatest strength lies where poverty and ignorance abound, so why do anything to endanger the institution?

It is surprising how few women voice objections to the degrading, humiliating role given them throughout the Bible. If a current publication ran similar degrading articles about women the condemnation would be loud and clear. Why the difference? Does this verify the effectiveness of brainwashing that begins at an early age? Or do many females just happen to be indifferent of their status?

For example, are women offended by Exodus 21:7–11, which explains how to sell a daughter? Leviticus 12:1–7 reports that a woman bearing a female child is considered unclean for sixty-six days, twice as long as bearing a male child. Keep in mind the difficulties humans had in maintaining cleanliness and sanitation in ancient times, since the loving, all-powerful, but mythical deity gave no hints about soap or hygiene. In fact, not until the religious suppression of the Dark Ages was broken were humans able to gradually educate themselves and improve living conditions and health. In addition to the religious rules listed above, after a woman gave birth she was denied the right to touch anything hallowed or to enter the sanctuary until her days of purification were fulfilled. Brainwashing works, for women have given far more to religion than males.

How much confidence should be given to a god who does not even explain the basics of reproduction to his children? When the alleged deity fails to inform them about the most basic necessities for cleanliness, how could women care for themselves during such difficult times as childbirth? Instead the Bible repeatedly refers to women as unclean. What would humans think of a parent who failed to give its offspring any information about life and no education? No religion has a deity that informed its believers about life, about the resources available in the world, how to develop those resources, or how to maintain good health. Surprised? You won't be if you recognize that religion is an organized power structure that maintains control through fear, threats, boycotts, and death to doubters.

On the matter of health, should women select a doctor and gynecologist who believes strictly in the Bible? An irrelevant question of course, for no medical services would exist for anyone if religion's domination had prevailed. Knowledge of the body was initially gained through secretly conducted autopsies, because religion's power structure strictly forbade this search for knowledge. What opposition could the church have had to this knowledge? If your belief is based on myths it is necessary and quite natural to deny anything that might weaken your belief. The lifestyle of humans in the developed world owes so much to the courageous people who risk severe punishment from religious authorities for daring to steal cadavers to study the anatomy of the human body. Today, what believer in religion really wants to live in the darkness that early religious authority tried to maintain?

The New Testament stories had to be gleaned from recollections given by people long after Jesus' death. That period was one of great turmoil, of many sects, splinter groups, even the destruction of the temple about 70 C.E. by the Romans. Even remnants relating to Jesus were considered heretical by the power structures. Nevertheless, the prevailing persecution seemed to prompt a flow of stories for years after Jesus' death. Paul's messages in the New Testament did not propose a centralized, authoritarian religion as existed in the established, dominant religions. Paul and Jesus believed individuals could speak to their God without paying and supporting intermediaries and that prophecy and teaching would be enough. However, humans seem to have a fondness for power structures. This weakens the hopes for a plain, unmistakably clear, participatory communication by individual with their deity. Rome's destruction of the Temple also dissolved any universal plan Paul had, and the center of the new cult was moved to Rome.

As previously noted, dozens of religious sects evolved in the first two or three centuries after Jesus' life, each claiming to have the true path. Paul's writing indicates the wide range of beliefs that existed, each claiming to be the words of Jesus. This confusion was handed down orally, generation after generation, resulting in wide variations in beliefs and customs. An Ophite group worshiped serpents, claiming the serpent triumphed over God. The book of 1 John introduced the confession as a defense to root out heresy and deviant beliefs. As to who was in charge, the men involved ran it as they saw fit, and, of course, women were subject to what men decreed. Fanatics gravitated to religion as noted in Matthew 19:12: "There are some who made themselves eunuchs for the kingdom of heaven's sake." Peter received more attention than Paul since Peter had been an apostle, though he denied Jesus when the chips were down. Constantine (ca. 280–337 C.E.) is claimed as a convert to Christianity. He did not receive baptism until on his deathbed, which dogma equates as remission of sins, and Constantine had plenty of sins. Superstition guided the man. He had a vicious temper with no respect for human life. As emperor he executed his eldest son, his second wife, and his favorite sister's husband. He probably embraced Christianity to suit his delusion of power, making a bargain with the church. His Milan Edict of tolerance to Christianity and paganism gave Constantine control of the church's policies. He put the rule of law ahead of religion, envisioning religion to be the role of a state.

From the first to fourth centuries the church changed from suffering, to begging for tolerance, to coercion, to a monopoly devised by the clerical staff. Gaining favors with government increased, as did pressure by special interests for appointments to key church positions. This evolved into such incidents as St. Ambrose being baptized, then moving through several clerical ranks, then being consecrated as bishop of Milan, all in eight days. Laypersons who were ordained directly to church positions included St. Augustine and St. Jerome. In 236 Fabian, a layperson, was elevated directly to pope. Bribery was common. Clerics became judges, drawing up wills and administering inheritances, even assigning the benefits to themselves. The authority and the wealth of the church grew, and the mythical God did not intervene.

From the third to the fifth centuries the number of monks increased, but largely from the ignorant, lower-class strata of society. The monasteries attracted misfits along with a few pious people. Gangs of monks formed, the black-robed monks smashing and burning the temples of opposing sects, as well as bullying, interfering with commerce, and engaging in class discrimination. The power of religious sects grew by using all the abuses known to man, including forged credentials and bribes to influence courts. Political empires of church and state faced similar problems, with the effect of drawing both institutions closer together.

Comparing the Old and New Testaments

❧

There is a close association between what is reported to be the ministry of Jesus and the Old Testament. However, the Old Testament has become an embarrassment to more moderate religious beliefs, because of the violence and depraved behavior it depicts. Today's clerics are careful in selecting passages from the Old Testament to avoid endorsing murder, incest, and deception. The New Testament's description of Jesus' message indicates that the general public had lost hope in the existing power structures. We do not know Jesus' exact message, but the biblical report is that he condemned oppressors, including Judaism and the occupying Roman government. According to the biblical writers, Jesus' message touched the minds and hearts of the masses, causing the oppressed—the desperate—to believe Jesus was the long-awaited messiah. Of course, human history records numerous cases of zealots becoming so wrapped up in their own story they begin to believe themselves to be clair-voyant, psychic, even possessing spiritual powers. To the oppressed, belief in a messiah was a ray of hope. With nothing written by Jesus, the evolving new power structure had a free hand to use material from the Old Testament to enhance the new myth. Quotes from the Old Testament like "not by bread alone" and crediting Jesus with miracles are taken from the Old Testament and work well in the New Testament story. Jesus' denial of being the messiah also comes from the Old Testament (Zechariah 13:5–6).

How authentic is the Old Testament with its legends handed down by ruling patriarchs? Today the Old Testament is not only an embarrassment to many religions, but historians consider the stories as questionable and an incomplete source of history. Egyptian history is considered more reliable and does not mention the biblical stories, nor does any other history reference mention the Bible stories. The Old Testament consists of laws, chronicles, genealogies, and prophesies alleged to be the word of the Lord in selecting the Israelites as his favorite people. It would be hard to improve on Steve Allen's description of the Old Testament in his book *The Bible, Religion, and Morality*:

> *The Old Testament portrait of Yahweh is too loutish and brutal to be worthy of worship by any theist who accepts the ethics of altruism, or that is familiar, even marginally, with modern science and biblical criticism. To find analogies with Yahweh one has to turn to the jealous, cruel, bloodthirsty gods of ancient mythologies.*
>
> *The proposition that the entire human race—consisting of hordes of humanity—would be placed seriously in danger of a fiery eternity, characterized by unspeakable torments purely because a man disobeyed a deity by eating a piece of fruit offered to him by his wife, is inherently incredible.*

Believers in religion have to reject reason and accept blind faith. For example, why a person of Abraham's character—a dishonorable, untrustworthy panderer—is revered by the Jews as an ancestor is a mystery. The story of Moses also poses a test of faith versus reason. At a much later time in history, Martin Luther's thoughts on faith versus reason were as follows: "Reason is the Devil's harlot who can do naught but slander and harm whatever God does or says." Fortunately, public opinion, though slow to act, can change religion, government, and societal standards. The hellfire-and-brimstone ministry that existed well into the nineteenth century finally gave way, as did the prohibition of eating certain foods and the right of women to serve as ministers in some religions. The personal freedom we often credit to democracy was to a great extent provided by the U.S. Constitution, which separates state and religion.

The commandments introduced in the Old Testament, consisting largely of prohibitions and bits of moral codes, plagiarized from Greek literature and advanced societies of western Asia that permeated into the remote areas occupied by the Israelite tribes. Though the tone and spirit of the New Testament is a major change over the Old Testament, neither secular nor religious segments of society in developed countries are concerned with upholding the commandment about killing. Think about the Crusades, the Inquisition, the thirty-year war in Europe, of Ireland, Kosovo, the Mideast, and Indonesia. The modern media only puts a different spin on the same human fallacies.

Judaism and Christianity have been fortunate that so few people read their Scriptures; the tradition's position on social issues is an embarrassment. Take Leviticus 25:44, which advises that slaves should come from the heathen class. Biblical leaders believed in exploiting those with different beliefs. Wars were a means of profiting from the wealth and captured slaves of the losers, and best of all the mythical deity was in on the deal. The winner's booty consisted of livestock, tools, jewelry, and women and children who could be sold as slaves. One of the rewards noted in Numbers 31 is thirty-two thousand virgins. In Judges 21:11 the victors collected four hundred young virgins. David, one of Israel's heroes, is credited with war booty of livestock and certain playthings. Then in 1 Samuel 27:9, his victory is described as follows: "He left neither man nor woman alive." Also consider this enlightened biblical policy: " [T]hen thou shalt let her go whither she will, but thou shalt not sell her at all for money," found in Deuteronomy 21:11–14. To become more enlightened read John 2:4, where Jesus shows his intolerance for women. His answer to request by his mother was, "Woman, what have I to do with thee?" Some modern biblical scholars view Jesus' remark as renouncing family, which is also affirmed in other alleged remarks by Jesus. Of course, Jesus wrote nothing, so we have to rely on what the spin doctors of that day decided was acceptable, which no doubt expressed the social standards that were appropriate for the time period.

The purpose of life and how it started is still unknown, unless you accept myths. Every religion had one or more. The insecurity felt by humans is a side effect of ignorance. Myths helped offset the drudgery and brutality of life for primitive people. Though many places on Earth have not advanced much beyond the primitive stage, people in developed nations have less reason for alarm or insecurity about life. Science provides so much information on the facets of life that intelligent people can find a niche, a purpose to make their lives meaningful and interesting. The productive mentality finds interest in the challenges and the opportunity to produce or provide items of value as a reward. The human brain permits humans to gain satisfaction from achievements. The myths of religions cause anxiety and delusions of horrible penalties if one does not subscribe to a totalitarian power structure that has only a mythical heaven to offer. Satisfaction and pleasures gained from the improved lifestyle that human intelligence provides exceeds by far the illusory promise of residing forever in a vague, ethereal location with no itinerary other than playing a harp and the obligation to flatter a deity that permits untold suffering on earth. Today the mentality of people living in developed nations is far more advanced than to believe the myth of humans created from a lump of dirt and the degrading role of women created from a man's rib.

After humans escaped from the oppression of religion that denied them education, life's purpose and challenge exploded in many directions. The educated mind recognizes the opportunities in the mathematical, biological, chemical, electromagnetic properties of Earth and a nascent universe. Though human knowledge in many fields is incomplete, such as theories about gravity or the genome, these unanswered questions no longer weigh heavily on most minds. We recognize by this time that humans are just one of many species, and except for myths, humans are not treated differently at death than any other species. It should concern us that the human species is one of the few to kill its own kind and that militarism continues to be one of the largest expenditures in our national budget. Humans also need to show concern for the planet's environment. Other species do not appear to be as destructive or as disruptive of an environmental balance.

WHY THE NEW TESTAMENT?

❧⦁❧

Paul's death is estimated to have occurred about 64 C.E. His letters were considered to be inspired and therefore were given special consideration when twenty-seven books were finally selected to represent the New Testament that was assembled in the fourth century. The Roman empire was collapsing, leaving Greek as the dominant language. Some biblical stories had to be translated, resulting in variations and causing dissension and discord. About 382 C.E. Pope Damascus authorized St. Jerome to revise what appeared to be conflicts in the New Testament that was adopted in 367, but this move did not end the debates. Some thought St. Jerome had injected Judaism. The disputes over St. Jerome's work did not die out until about the seventh century. Were the divinely inspired authors tuned to the wrong channel, or did the mythical deity enjoy dissension? As late as the sixteenth century, this debate lingered and resulted in every European country translating the Scriptures into their own language. By this time questions on the authenticity or purity of alleged revelations could not be settled, because no reliable eyewitnesses were ever provided to give testimony. Doubts arose as to whether or not to believe that mystics and seers really had an inner road to truth. Such questions probably remain unanswered today, but the concern has disappeared because so few people read the Bible and have largely relegated religion to a social function. Most people are not concerned with the authenticity of the Bible, nor are they about to challenge something that matters so little to them. This indifference offers safety for religion, but as for the people, "those who do not remember history are condemned to repeat it."

Scholars of biblical history consider the Gospel of Mark as the earliest of the first four Gospels, appearing about 70 C.E., about thirty years after Jesus' death. The Gospels of Matthew, Luke, and John came later and are judged to have appeared between 80 and 100 C.E.. These four Gospels were later selected to be the foundation of the New Testament. The Gospels were written by persons not personally acquainted with Jesus. Take into account the time lapse and the lack of records in that time period, and the work has the status of hearsay. Not until 367, more than three hundred years after Jesus' death, did the bishops of Alexandria select twenty-seven documents, declaring them to be the New Testament. Although wide and significant differences exist in the four principal Gospels, the authority of Christianity's hierarchy claimed that all authors were divinely inspired.

An event that happened about this time illustrates the intolerance religion has always exhibited for any different belief or opinions. Around 385 C.E. Christians destroyed the temples of the competing religions of Mithra, Dionysius, and the Ptolemaic religion that were some seven centuries older than Christianity. They also destroyed the large collection of classical literature and manuscripts of science, history, and philosophy dating back to the time of Alexander the Great. What motivated Christianity to destroy this history? If your belief is based on myths, then tolerance of competition, knowledge, and reason that might weaken your myth is difficult. Even modern dictators tend to destroy the people and the work associated with higher education. During the sixteenth century, the Spanish conquistadors as emissaries of Christianity destroyed what appear to have been highly civilized societies in Mexico and Peru. Also during the sixteenth century, Christianity killed and plundered the wealth of many indigenous people of Central and South America, and reparations have never been paid to those nations or their people—unless, of course, some people might consider Pope John Paul II's recent canonizing of indigenous Mexican peasant Juan Diego, who was alleged to have seen an apparition of the Virgin of Guadalupe in the year 1531, as just compensation for a nation plagued with poverty for centuries. Somehow the power structure gets off easy; institutionalized fear seems to mesmerize.

MYTHS HAVE A LONG SHELF LIFE

꩜

A new cult's success in biblical times required a story capable of competing with existing exotic and mystical stories. Ignorance and superstitions provided the ideal incubation climate for myths and cults. One established religion existing when biblical stories were forming was the Persian Mithraism. It had an existing structure of priests; a worship ceremony using bells, candles, and holy water; and a ritual that included consecrated bread in communion services. Does all of that sound familiar? The Mithraic deity also assumed the power to define blasphemy, which was punishable by death. It took over a thousand years for humans to acquire the knowledge and a system of justice to tame the violence approved by their deities. Most civil societies now have laws prohibiting the violence found in the Bible. Until educated societies developed courts and justice, the Christian hierarchy burned nonbelievers at the stake, even as late as the sixteenth century. Religion introduced ethnic cleansing early in history. Excommunication by religion's hierarchy was used to mark opponents for punishment in an afterlife, of which no proof exists, but is supported by fear and hearsay.

Though Christianity denies evolution, its devotion practices have evolved by adopting pagan beliefs. For example, December 25, selected to celebrate Jesus' birthday, was copied from the pagan Mithraic holiday of Sol Invictus (the sun) and was celebrated with gifts and festivals. Mithras, according to some myths, was born from a rock and witnessed by several shepherds who brought gifts and adored him. Other myths claimed Mithras was born of a virgin in a cave in midwinter. Mithras also performed miracles; during a drought he shot an arrow into a rock causing water to flow. The biblical story has Moses doing likewise by striking a rock. Mithraism held Sunday sacred and December 25 the sun's holiday. Their religion encouraged celibacy, and virgins served God in a heaven where all men were judged. Women are not mentioned, but Christians also dismissed them. Mithraism believed in immortality, the resurrection of the flesh, a fiery destruction of the world, and celebrated the atoning death of Mithras and his resurrection. With a little knowledge of history, one can see how the Bible came into being. Ancient stories became legends passed along orally for centuries until such time as written languages evolved. The new Christian cult could easily copy from others as there was no penalty or offense for plagiarizing myths.

Currently used religious symbols and devices that were copied from much earlier religion include the rosary, the scapular, candles, holy water, oils, and incense, all traceable to ancient people and their creeds. Remnants of exorcism even exist in the currently used rituals of burning incense, serving Communion, chanting, and blessing bells, crosses, and medals. Pagan religions believed incense smoked out demons, a practice and belief that exists in some religions today. A more logical reason for introducing the use of incense into a religious ceremony in biblical times may have been to serve as a deodorant. No religion has a god that ever passed along the knowledge to its believers on any of life's essentials such as soap or how to provide running water in dwellings. A room full of the unwashed could conceivably have quite an odor. A cult leader trying to clinch and extend his power structure and possibly gaining financial support like an annuity from everyone could hardly say, "My God, this place stinks." Instead he introduced incense, and voila! Rather than insult the audience, he invented another myth, and incense gained the power to chase evil spirits. One can understand this working on the ignorant masses in millennia past, but to find it still in use and believed today is a serious indictment on human intelligence.

Incense is not the only ancient practice to influence religion. Ancient Egyptians believed a story of Osiris and Isis, the latter being goddess of fertility. She was usually represented with cow's horns surrounded by a lunar disc. Osiris was god of the dead in this popular myth. He was also the eldest son of the Earth god Geb and the sky goddess Nut. Osiris's wife, Isis, happened to be his sister, which was not a problem for a myth. To make the story as interesting as a modern TV program, Osiris had a jealous brother Seth who coveted being king; therefore, Seth killed Osiris. Does this remind you a bit of the biblical story of Cain and Abel? Seth places Osiris's body in a coffin and sets it floating down the Nile. As the story goes, the coffin reached the coast of Lebanon. The distraught Isis searched far and wide, finally located the coffin and body, and returned the entire package to Egypt. Seth was not about to be defeated; he dismembered Osiris's body and scattered the parts over the countryside. That still is not end of the story. Isis began another search and finally collected all the body parts of Osiris. Next comes the Mother of All Myths: With Osiris's body parts collected, Isis succeeds in impregnating herself—using the essential parts of Osiris's body—and produces son Horus, who becomes the ruler of the living.

As stories go, that tale offers real competition to immaculate conception. Of course you need to know that Isis derived her magic power from the sun god Ra. The strength of the cult's popularity came from including the myth of an afterlife. Of course, that story still has good sales appeal, though the writers of the Old Testament failed to mention an afterlife. The New Testament saw its value, though, and reinstated it. Egyptians also expected to be judged after death and to be presented to Osiris for judgment. "I am the resurrected and the life"—the phrase found in the Bible—is copied from an Egyptian chant for their god Osiris, the judge of the dead. To the uneducated masses without a clue regarding their own purpose in life, or about any part of the world about them, the myth served as a crutch. The ancients had a myth for almost everything they did not understand. For that matter, many people still classify anything they do not understand as a miracle. For that reason among others, angels still come in handy.

The early Romans also had myths. An important one was about Romulus and Remus as the legendary founders of Rome. In this story twin sons are born to the vestal virgin Rhea Sylvia. They were fathered by the god Mars, which is a slight variation to immaculate conception. In this myth the infant twins are thrown into the Tiber River by Amulius, who usurped Rhea's father's throne. Myths served well for pregnant unwed ladies to escape the social stigma that has continued in society until just recently. The abandoned twins of the virgin Rhea Sylvia drifted to shore where a she-wolf suckled the babes until they were discovered and raised by a herdsman. When the boys reached adulthood they sought revenge (a common emotion in biblical stories), killed Amulius, and restored their grandfather to his throne.

As young men Romulus and Remus decided to build a city but found they could not agree upon a location. They decided to rely upon omens or signs to resolve this matter. (Sound logical for good city planning?) Remus is the first to report an omen; he dreamed of six vultures. Romulus easily tops that, claiming a dream of twelve vultures. Romulus won and starts to build a city on Palatine Hill. Apparently Romulus had a sense of guilt for topping the dream of vultures and, taking no chances, he kills Remus. This may also have set the pattern for the biblical writers of the Old Testament where Cain kills Abel. The myth is about the construction of Rome that began in 753 B.C. Like most myths this one portrays human nature. The success of Romulus begins to attract questionable types, and Rome becomes a refuge for outlaws. The women in the near-by city of Selmes are being kidnapped by underworld Roman hoods. Romulus recognizes his reputation is important, so he gains identity with Quirinus, an early god of war, and proceeds to conquer the Sabine tribe of central Italy. This tells you that wars were used even in early times to deflect attention from local problems. This myth established the paternity of Romulus and Remus, tracing it to Mars, thus giving the Romans a feeling of superiority to their neighbors. Self-esteem was important back in pre-Christian times as well!

The number of myths created for the uninformed, primitive, and superstitious people was endless. Of course, myths served to fill vacuums, the black hole of human ignorance. A later myth would have you believe stories of a loving, all-powerful deity that picked the Israelites as his favorites and helped them wage war against those with different beliefs (sort of like Catholics and Protestants in Ireland, Jews and Palestinians in the so-called Holy Land, Hindus and Muslims, and on and on). Can the ability to create myths be considered a positive stimulus? Greek mythology served to cover all bases; they had a myth for almost everything and may have played a part in making the Greek nation a leader among Mediterranean nations for several centuries. For example, the Greek god of memory was Mnemosyne, mother of the muses who in turn presided over literature, the arts, and sciences. Their supreme deity was Zeus, son of Cronus and Rhea who also happened to be Zeus's sister. To the Romans Zeus was known as Jupiter and as Dyans Pita to Asian Indians. The many myths became intertwined, but credit should be given to these early humans for designing what is known as a power structure, thus creating an ascending hierarchy of gods. Power structures may have helped to confront the untamed world surrounding early humans. After they reach the top of their mythical genealogy chart of gods, a void still remained that had to be filled with blind faith, like modern religion. These early residents with their myths did as well as the biblical authors who also had no explanation of where God came from or where he obtained the elements and materials to make the universe. At that point it is like answering a child's question by saying, "You have to believe!"

The Zeus myth is quite exceptional; he fathered several other gods from his wife and his 115 mistresses, producing 140 offspring. His children ranked as Olympian divinities. From an incestuous affair with his mother he fathered Persephone, whom Hades myth, he abducted to be his wife and to live in the underworld. Then Zeus, with his daughter Persephone, fathered Dionysus, making that a double incestuous relation. Dionysus is referred to as the tyrant of Syracuse and as the god of viticulture, with the duty to wander and teach wine making. The myth has him attending frenzied wine celebrations with troupes of nymphs in religious orgies that were also attended by women who roamed the mountains dressed in fawn skirts, shrieking, brandishing torches, and eating raw flesh by tearing live animals apart.

The resurrection of the dead was a common theme in ancient myths, so how could the New Testament leave it out of the story? Another Greek myth intended for imagery to influence public thought is that of Orpheus, a poet-musician, son of Apollo, who descends into the underworld to lead his wife Eurydice back from the dead. She was fatally bitten by a snake as she tried to escape the advances of Aristieus, also Apollo's son. Orpheus failed to rescue Eurydice when he broke one of the rules in Hades, namely, the prohibition to look back. Orpheus and Eurydice were near to escaping Hades when Orpheus looked back to see if his wife was following, and this caused her to disappear. Do you suppose this myth had anything to do with Lot's wife as she and Lot were escaping the destruction the Lord caused in Sodom and Gomorrah? Lot's poor wife disobeyed the Lord's command; she looked back, and the Lord, demonstrating his infinite compassion, turned her into a pillar of salt. That story took just a minor alteration to add it to the Bible, and clearly it makes as much sense as the Greek story of Orpheus. It is apparent that storytellers copied each others' work.

The remaining part of the Orpheus myth does not have a happy ending either. He died as a guest of Thracian women who were performing mystic rites in celebration of Dionysus. Enraged at Orpheus's unwillingness to participate, the women tore him apart, throwing his head into the river Hebrus. As the head drifted down river it continued to cry out for Eurydice. The head finally beached at the island of Lesbos where an oracle lived, and the Orpheus lyre was placed in the sky and is known as the constellation Lyra. One has to admit the creative minds of ancients seem equal to our twentieth- and twenty-first century television programs. The central theme of these early myths provided models for the biblical authors who wrote several hundred years later, though they were declared to be divinely inspired. A righteous life became a requirement to cleanse life's impurities. Death was viewed as an essential step to release the soul, allowing it to escape to a mythical paradise. It seems in all the stories that the impure and unrepentant have always been destined to writhe in hell or Hades. However, no logical reason explains why the biblical leaders, the few who talked with God—like Abraham, Moses, David, Joshua—were murderers and had numerous wives and concubines, and yet they are the heroes of religion.

Note that incest is a common occurrence in myths and must have been accepted. It does seem a bit strange that the divinely inspired authors of the Bible did not get the message regarding incest and the consequences from the loving, all-powerful, all-knowing deity. Again, humans had to learn that lesson by trial and error. Incest also appears in early Egyptian history, and apparently this did not present a problem for authors of the Old Testament. The entire subject was apparently so unimportant that the Bible's creation story did not bother to create another female to be Cain's wife. Unless one takes the modern stand of "Don't ask, don't tell," one can assume that Cain had incestuous relations with Eve, his mother, for she was the only female around at the time. This relationship exists in early myths. Then in the Bible story of Lot, he sleeps with his two daughters. This does not seem to be a popular passage for clerics to read from the pulpit or to be recommended for family reading.

It would be hard to deny that the abundance of myths that existed for centuries did not influence the stories created as early religions began to form, including the cult that became Christianity. For centuries, the Greek myths about how the world began were believed and no doubt influenced writings for centuries. The Zeus myth begins with his father Cronus fearing he would be overthrown by his children. For this reason, Cronus adopted the practice of swallowing them as newborn babies. Rhea, the wife of Cronus, who was also his sister, decided to save her unborn child by wrapping a stone in swaddling clothes. Cronus swallowed the stone, believing it to be Zeus. The baby was then sent to the island of Crete and hidden in a cave. The myth has the infant Zeus cared for by nymphs and nourished by a goat and honey gathered from bees. Weapon clattering provided by semidivine beings danced around the babe to prevent Cronus the father from hearing the cries of Zeus.

When Zeus became an adult, he had several wives, including named Hera, or Lady, who happened to be his sister. He also had 115 mistresses, both mortal and immortal. The myths of Zeus covered every phase of life, an indication that insecure humans compensated by providing myths to serve as security blankets. Not surprisingly, centuries later when biblical stories were written, similar themes or episodes appeared, like Joseph and Mary taking baby Jesus to Egypt because the Roman administrator Herod decided to kill all male babies. However, it is odd that only a few of the New Testament Gospels used that story, and neither Roman nor Egyptian history mentions the biblical trip Joseph, Mary, and baby Jesus made to Egypt. It is also recognized that Roman and Egyptian history are considered more accurate than the Bible stories. God sure lacked knowledge of the value of public relations.

The popular Greek myth of Hercules includes his rising from the dead as smoke from Mt. Olympus. The smoke rose to the heavens and became the constellation Hercules. It would be expected that biblical stories would at least match the imagination and color of the myths existing at the time. It was common for Roman heroes to rise into the heavens after death and not uncommon for famous men to be born of women who had been impregnated by a god. The Greek myth of Adonis, a beautiful lover of Venus, died and rose each year. Custom and tradition would almost require any new story to include bringing the dead back to life. In every country that Christianity entered beliefs in dead heroes being resurrected by a god already existed. Mesopotamians had Tammuz, the Chaldeans had Ur, and the Persians had Attis of Mithraism. Certainly a person should have the right to choose whatever belief or myths were deemed necessary to support them in life. That freedom is not the problem. Problems arise when believers of religions, cults, or myths demand that everyone else must hold the same beliefs. This attitude has started many wars—and still does for that matter.

By coordinating archaeology and bits of ancient history, it has been possible to trace religious dogma and beliefs. For many people it is easier, and possibly safer, to accept whatever belief seems to be popular, an action known as the wisdom of numbers or following the herd. The Bible story carefully omits that the human species arrived on Earth with no knowledge of itself, of its purpose, or even the smallest bit of the problems to be faced in the world. Even the inquiring mind of Pythagoras, the Greek philosopher and mathematician born 570 B.C. whose name is associated with geometry, concluded that the universe started from a seed that grew as it sucked in pneuma or air, a name among several that ultimately became the word "soul," which also remains undefined today. Another early thinker, Empedocile, born around 490 B.C. on the island of Sicily, decided everything consisted of four elements: earth, fire, air, and water. No evidence shows that the biblical deity, or any other deity devised by humans in their long history, ever attempted to correct the mistaken logic or reasoning of humans. In fact, the error regarding the four elements proposed by Empedocile was later accepted by Aristotle and was virtually unchallenged until late into the seventeenth and eighteenth centuries. Why could so much time elapse before an error of this magnitude would be discovered? Keep in mind that one major obstacle to learning has always been custom and tradition. Add to that the drag caused by individuals choosing the easy path of accepting the majority view, and add to that the opposition of religion. Credit needs to be given to Pythagoras for arriving at the belief that more existed in the cosmos than could be seen. This did not make him popular with the general public, which felt comfortable with believing Earth was flat. With religion's opposition to education for a millennium or more, the smothering cloud of ignorance prevailed.

THE STATUS QUO HOLDS

∽o∾

Humans existed for millennia without the benefit of a written language. Any deity with an ounce of vision or thought would have recognized the stifling effect of illiteracy on human progress. Alphabetic writing did not begin in Greece until about the eighth century B.C. and had achieved only limited use by the sixth century B.C. A cuneiform writing on clay tablets was developed in Mesopotamia around 3200 B.C., but according to the Bible these were not God's favorite children. The lack of an accessible media certainly restricted learning and the inability to pass knowledge to the next generation. Mythical deities could not resolve a handicapped media. Fortunately, most species are capable of learning, and the few rare humans who persisted in the search for answers could be considered the beginning of our data bank. A scientific approach is not deterred or intimidated by failure; stagnation occurs when religion and politics restrict thought and experimentation in order to protect their myths and/or limited vision.

Several Greeks were among those trying to decipher and to give meaning to their surroundings. A few are credited with the beginning of philosophy and mathematics. One early assumption was that the world had the power to grow or develop on its own, and this ability provided change rather than the creation out of nothing by gods. Several early thinkers recognized that growing things required air and water. The epic poet Homer, author of the Iliad and the Odyssey about 800 B.C., recognized these fundamentals. Air in particular was recognized as a key, the breath of life or *psuche*. They knew air escaped upon death, and the word evolved to mean "soul." Another example of the state of ignorance comes from a writing of the Roman Hippolytus in the third century C.E. He wrote ". . . the heavenly bodies do not move under the earth, but around it, and the sun is not hidden under the earth but is covered by the higher part of the earth." The absence of any understanding of the world indicates how easy it was for the creators of mythical deities to develop and impose a power structure.

Another peculiar early belief was that Poseidon, the Greek god of the sea and horses, caused earthquakes. The Roman god Neptune was included in these early earth and sun theories. About 350 B.C. the philosopher Aristotle suggested that earthquakes occurred when the earth dried out and pieces broke off. He based this on his observation of cracks in earth caused by droughts. It becomes apparent how difficult the learning process was from the beginning with no help from any mythical deity. The role of the god myths was to create power structures and keep things intact with threats of damnation. As religions evolved, support came from the public's ignorance of the Scriptures, since only the clergy were permitted to read and interpret it. The tithe of 10 percent levied on income set as religion's standard made the power structure extremely wealthy—

hardly what Jesus had in mind—but was not discouraged by Christianity.

The history of humans, regardless of their location on planet Earth, has a common theme of searching for the meaning and purpose of life, a life that was generally brutal and short. Thousands of years would pass before ancient hieroglyphics would be replaced with alphabets. Many of the early writings consisted of setting into print the legends created by patriarchs, and these were about God talking to his favorites, the Israelites. For instance, in Ezekiel 43:7 God says, "I will dwell in the midst of the children of Israel forever." In Jeremiah 4:7 God expresses his preference for Jews, saying, "Saith the Lord, the lion is come up from his thicket and the destroyer of the Gentiles is on his way." The Bible leaves little doubt that God was a coconspirator in murder and that the Old Testament was written to justify the military exploits of the Israelite tribes. Not until the New Testament was any other group of people, the Gentiles, even considered, and then only because the promoters, Paul and party, could not sell their new cult to the Jews. If you give this a second thought, does this seem a likely path to peace? It hasn't happened yet, after thousands of years, though the mythical God they created is alleged to be all-powerful.

Who were the so-called divinely inspired authors, and did they represent a special interest? Preparing for wars and conquests has always been a major undertaking for humans, and remains so to this day. The purpose of the spin doctor has always been to get public acceptance for some event that needs financial support by the public and possibly physical support as well. Religion has never shied away from supporting military force, as documented by history and the current imbroglios found in Ireland, the former Yugoslavia, Afghanistan, Iran, Iraq, parts of India, and Indonesia. If you examine the military engagements around the world, religion is the divisive tool that whets the hate needed to instigate wars and thus justify astronomical expenditures for military hardware. Even in spite of the remarkable advancement in knowledge made by humans in what is termed the developed world, military preparedness and expenditures are unabated almost everywhere. For some strange reason the people in the developed part of the world do not recognize that their personal freedom and security has continued to erode each time our military presence is extended around the world.

The Bible does not tell how the large armies were recruited century after century as the mythical deity's leaders carried out conquests and looting. Biblical stories refer to armies ranging in size of from tens of thousands to hundreds of thousands of soldiers. How did they communicate to assemble and then direct such vast numbers of men? How did they arm them? Imagine if you can, the gore, the butchery, and the slaughter of virtually hand-to-hand conflict with clubs, spears, knives, and the like. God had to like violence. How were these armies financed? Can you imagine the tax levied to support such huge armies? No wonder the tax man was detested. If the army lived off the land, would there have been anything left for the homeowner? No one mentioned caring for the dead and wounded. As for the biblical stories of these events, they were orally passed from patriarch to patriarch for centuries, until writing was finally invented. The power structure had to convince an ever-passing parade of humans of the heroics of war heroes and to also maintain belief in the mythical deity.

The power of the religious myths is illustrated in the current dispute in the so-called Holy Land, though few have the courage and basic honesty to address the problem. Nothing has really changed. Religious myths have been the basis for much human violence. For some reason, though, many people believe religion is the precursor to peace. The feeling of compassion in humans is easily overruled when the power structure decides to activate the inherent desire of humans to kill their own kind.

HANDLE WITH CARE

⚬

A dominant characteristic of humans is fear. Note how the Lord exploits this in Deuteronomy 13:3–10: "[L]ove with all your heart and all your soul," but if you even dream of, think about, or listen to another deity, "thou shall kill whoever proposes such. . . . Thine hand shall be first upon him to put him to death. . . . Thou shall stone him, that he die, because he hath sought to thrust thee away from the Lord." This loving God did not intend to permit the idea of democracy or free speech. Loving your enemy, or in the Old Testament, loving thy neighbor, was pure rhetoric that no one was expected to follow. In fact, there seems to be a void in these biblical attitudes. Is there only love or dislike or hate? Suppose one has a neutral position and only upholds that justice and fairness be meted out to all? There should be little question why slavery, serfdom, and oppression of every sort existed for millennia while religion maintained its totalitarian power. Freedom does not exist today in governments dominated by religion.

Clerics carefully avoid another side to the myth of the loving God when suggesting Scripture reading. For instance, in Malachi 2:3, the Lord says: "Behold, I will corrupt your seed, and spread dung upon your faces, even the dung of your solemn feasts." Another unwholesome bit can be found in Ezekiel 4:12: "And thou shall eat it as barley cakes and thou shall bake it with dung that cometh out of man in their sight." Then Deuteronomy 28:53 has a long list of curses that this same loving God will impose on any who do not follow his commands, including, "And thou shall eat the fruit of thine own body, the flesh of thy sons and daughters. . . . " Perhaps this opened the way for cannibalism. Myths cannot withstand close examination and reason. Hence, religion has to rely on institutionalized fear.

Judaism is founded on the Old Testament, which is alleged to have been written by divine revelation. The arrogance of claiming to be God's chosen people has made them a target for persecution and untold suffering. Even a casual observer of current world conditions can see that religious beliefs are a major cause of conflict and destruction. It should also be obvious how difficult it is to modify beliefs that are indoctrinated from birth. The history of Judaism extends over a long period of time. Jews were conquered and enslaved at different times by Assyrians and Babylonians, exposing them to the Babylonian story of a great flood. This exaggerated story came in handy when the Jews got around to writing their own mythical story. When establishing Islam in the seventh century, Mohammed's armies killed great numbers of Jews. A few centuries later Christianity amassed armies several times over a period of nearly three centuries, invading the eastern Mediterranean area to kill infidels—namely, Muslims who held a different belief. In the thirteenth century, Christianity introduced ethnic cleansing of Jews and Moors in what is known as the Spanish Inquisition. Though burning people at the stake is barbaric, this was approved by the Catholic hierarchy with the consent of the Spanish king and queen. Thousands of Jews and Moors were eliminated, people who had lived peacefully together in Spain for centuries until Christianity came along.

Does religion pose a conundrum? If you believe the Old Testament and use that as starting point, the Israelites were promised a messiah who would establish a new kingdom of Zion. According to Joel 3:15–20: "The Lord shall roar out of Zion, and utter his voice from Jerusalem and the heavens and earth shall shake. . . . Judah shall dwell forever and Jerusalem from generation to generation." That forecast was slightly in error as Judah was captured some twenty-six hundred years later and the Romans sacked Jerusalem, destroying the temple in 70 C.E.. One can understand that Judaism, based on the Old Testament, and its claim of being God's chosen people could be sold to ignorant tribes in the times before Jesus, but to be believed today by otherwise intelligent people is beyond belief, until you recognize the power structure behind it. Of course, the Jews are not alone in holding arrogant and selfish beliefs. There are others who also claim to have the only true religion and speak with forked tongues on war and peace. The divisive nature of religion inflames emotions and justifies killing fellow human beings, as is clearly demonstrated in numerous spots around the world.

Today, few who claim to be believers have thoroughly studied Scripture, history, or modern archaeological findings. Hence, it appears inevitable that the public will support continued wars and expenditures for religious structures, though this is contrary to the biblical description of Jesus.

A Continuing Thread

The structure adopted by early cults and now a part of established religion has a thin vein indicative of a desperate search for the meaning of the life. The prevailing and unanswered questions are as follows: Why are we here and what is our purpose? The knowledge that now exists in developed nations had its beginning from a few early and exceptional individuals who kept searching for a meaning to life. Gradually, the ability to reason, inquire, compare, analyze, theorize, and debate produced knowledge. Humans were forced to start with nothing; no loving creator left a thing. The myths developed by the cunning, the warlords who faked conversations with mythical deities, were a counterintelligent force that created havoc for its own gain. Life to the majority was a blind alley. The way out did not lie with myths, for dependence on myths prevents real knowledge from entering, as demonstrated by the slow progress of the human species. The biblical authors, claiming to be divinely inspired, were ignorant of the physical, biological, astronomical, geological, and chemical nature of the universe.

Think what even a hint by the allegedly loving deity of the Periodic Table of elements would have done to advance the lifestyle of humans!

If one applies even simple logic to the book of Genesis, one must ask why would God first create a dark chaos and then spend six days putting the chaotic condition back into order? Whatever the origin of the human species, we stand apart from all other species with such achievements as the discovery and mapping of the genetic code. This knowledge has the potential for advancing health and a lifestyle beyond anything previously experienced in human existence. History and archaeology have brought to light the similarities in the human species regardless of where they lived. Though separated by thousands of miles, similarities exist in human history, whether in the Mediterranean civilizations or the Aztec nation in Central America. The religions of humans were a divisive force, because of the control of power structures.

VIOLENCE ON A LOCAL SCALE

∽∘∾

Communion in an Aztec celebration consisted of making an image of their holy deity out of dough into which the blood of an infant had been kneaded. The dough was divided and consumed by the participants. For the annual feast honoring the Aztec deity, an individual was selected to represent the deity, and after suitable rites the individual was sacrificed. Special dignitaries ate the arms and legs and the remaining flesh was chopped up and distributed among the common people. When the Spaniards invaded and reached Mexico City in 1519 they reported finding a pyramid of skulls beside the Aztecs temple. They learned that thirty-three years earlier at the Aztec's great Huitzilopochtli festival, a dedication for the son of the Sun God, at least seventy thousand victims were sacrificed in this mythical deity's honor.

Meanwhile Christianity finally conceded that the world was not flat, and that Earth was not the center of the universe with every other celestial bit rotating around it. This concession came too late for a few courageous pioneers who pursued reason and assembled facts about celestial bodies. An apology by religion for its mistaken beliefs and the violence used against those seeking knowledge was a long time coming. As late as 1600 the Vatican burned philosopher Bruno at the stake for expressing his belief that Earth was not alone, that a number of worlds existed in the universe. In 1633 Galileo also challenged the Vatican's view on astronomy; for this he was forced to kneel before the Inquisitional Tribunal of Rome and renounce his belief in the Copernican theory of the universe. To further protect the ignorant masses from such enlightened thought the Vatican placed Galileo under house arrest for the last eight years of his life. No deity came to the rescue of these early scientists.

Christianity's hierarchy suppressed knowledge and enlightenment for fear of losing control. Eventually the Vatican was unable to maintain a state of ignorance, to suppress the desire of motivated persons searching for knowledge. The mathematics of the Copernican theory became the foundation of our modern space programs. Men like Galileo, Descartes, and Kepler provided the groundwork for the evolution in science, making computers and the Internet possible. As for Copernicus, the Vatican excommunicated him, showing no compassion as Jesus might have done. The myth of creation offered nothing to advance knowledge—no biological, chemical, geological, electrical, or astronomical information, nor any mention of the important theories on gaseous and electrical fields that are so important in our current standard of living.

It does not take long for a person to recognize that inequalities exist in life along with the slings and arrows to be endured. This uncertainty makes many people perfect subjects to exploit with fear of the unknown, particularly where emotional and physical pain is associated with death. Christianity does not mention that the Old Testament does not promise an afterlife. Nor did the Old Testament suggest that the dead would rise again. Note Ecclesiastes 3:19–20: "For what befalleth the sons of man . . . befalleth beasts. . . . As the one dieth, so dieth the other. All goeth into one place; all are the dust and all turn to dust again." However, fear of death was too valuable a weapon for the power structure not to turn the event into a means of control.

We do not know when the suggestion of an afterlife and immortality was introduced into religious belief. Early Jewish sects even opposed the idea. At some point the religions of Asia filtered into Arab and Mediterranean areas, and the idea of an afterlife spread, though it is supported only by hearsay. In the sixth or seventh century B.C., religious teacher Zoroaster, a Persian who founded Zoroastrianism, claimed that compartments could be found in the final resting place for humans, a sort of popular refinement. The righteous would be separated from the wicked, with the deity Yahweh presiding over the good, and the devil over the wicked. By the year 2 B.C., the apocryphal book of Enoch had expanded the final resting place into four compartments to make room for friends. The wicked and the damned really lost support; their final resting place became a hot spot when descriptions of burning and boiling were added. Several hundred years later, when the Bible was being assembled, people could draw from a number of sources or models. If you read the book of Revelation, you can find really wild hallucinations that added descriptions of monsters and brimstone. Even then people liked an exciting story.

Almost from birth the uninformed and religious implant the fear of the unknown, and this continues until death. Religion's myths are also aided by the ego of humans who believe they are superior to all other animals, though humans are one of the few species that kill their own kind and commit acts of cruelty not known to other species. Religion is further assisted by the fact that no communication can occur between earthlings and the mythical heaven and hell. Those who do not apply reason are likely to be permanently indoctrinated with fear. Only in the last two hundred years or less have the more alert minds applied reason and logic as science has opened up the potential of the universe and the contradictions of religion. These achievements required the freedom to explore science. No evidence shows the mythical, loving god, invented by cults and religions, ever assisting with tapping the resources of the universe.

No biblical writings, on stone or other medium, ever offered the slightest hint of how to achieve the knowledge to release humans from their miserable, primitive lifestyle. What caring parents would treat their offspring with such indifference? What parents would choose to deny their children the educational opportunities that humans finally developed during the last century, enhancing health and employment opportunities? Our knowledge of the universe has reduced death and injuries from natural disasters in our chaotic world. The mythical God left not even a hint for humans regarding such natural disasters as wind, rain, floods, lightning, and earthquakes.

Freedom of Thought–The Difference

After centuries of suffering imposed by religion an important crack appeared in the power structure, letting in a ray of light. It was the invention of the movable type by the German printer Gutenberg about the year 1450. The stranglehold on education held for millennia by religion was broken. Productivity in printing, books, literature, and particularly the Bible released individuals to thought and reason. Until this time Christianity's hierarchy opposed commoners having access to the Bible. Only clerics were permitted to interpret the Bible, and they were often ignorant and dishonest. An example of religion's paranoia occurred when Englishman William Tyndale began translating and printing the Bible in English. The clergy, Christianity's power structure, confiscated and burned Tyndale's work. Tyndale fled to Europe to continue his work, but he was pursued, captured, and burned at the stake by his critics. The power structure of Christianity used whatever force was necessary to preserve their monopoly and thought control.

Centuries passed before humans could accumulate the scientific and mechanical knowledge to reduce drudgery and improve the lifestyle. A reasoning person would surely ask, why would a loving deity, as claimed by religion, do nothing for Earth's early residents? But then, what has modern religion done to relieve the horrors of modern wars, to assist the poor and alleviate starvation? The loss of life and property by natural disasters continues to this day, with no alerts or information coming from the mythical deity. Any assistance on this subject had to wait for science to provide answers.

KEEP IT THE SAME

∞○∞

Custom and tradition are difficult to change. Why do church steeples point toward the sky? Steeples date back to pagan designs of ceremonial altars and pyramids. To early humans the sky was a mystery. They believed objects like the stars were relatively close, rather than light years away as science has determined. The beauty and mystery of numerous unknown objects in the sky provided dreams of a peaceful existence in some soft, puffy location in the sky. At least dreams could stimulate the hope that offset the difficult lives of primitive humans. Hence pointing a religious symbol toward the sky enhanced the dream that a better life existed somewhere. To a struggling, ignorant person with no idea of why he or she existed in a chaotic world a clean, blue sky stirred the dreams of a peaceful place to rest. To the charlatan or the sorcerer, these illusions offered the ideal framework for deception and control. It was easy to capitalize on and exploit misfortune and disappointments, and that tactic has not changed much. Today the lives of billions of "God's children" still need the solace and comfort of dreams of some imaginary place to escape poverty, anxiety, illness, and drudgery.

Surprisingly few people who suffer from any number of a long list of maladies ever associate or accuse their deity of being responsible for creating diseases and human bodies that are susceptible to malfunctions. No mention is made in the so-called divinely inspired Scriptures on how to provide even basic items like soap, clean water, toilet paper, pain relievers, or plants that can provide antidotes to some illnesses. The divinely inspired Scriptures do not offer even a hint about the simplest concepts in science, like the wheel, the wedge, the lever, or magnetism and electricity. No religion gave clues on health, sanitation, or a warning that exposure to the Sun causes cancer. Religion is a power structure that the wily and clever create to control the masses, and the technique has served well.

Religions are purely power structures that institutionalize fear as a weapon for controlling and extracting wealth from a vast number of people. The best defense for humans against being exploited is to search for knowledge and by trial and error. Of course, this method of learning can be hazardous; the natural laws are unforgiving, and they are not mentioned in the Bible. If religion's loving, all-powerful, all-knowing God really did exist, why didn't he/she/it offer instructions on how to provide pure drinking water, show where resources are located, or at least list the chemical elements randomly scattered on Earth? Even today more than a billion people do not have safe drinking water, and it does not bother the mythical deity. What would humans do today to a father who created something so insidious as poison ivy without telling his children of the consequences?

The World Health Organization estimates that twenty-five thousand people die daily from water-related illnesses. If the creation story is correct, then God created malaria, the virus that infects an estimated five hundred thousand to one million new cases every year. The disease is so common that the death toll is difficult to assess, but an estimated one million people die annually of the disease. Most of those victims are children. Malaria is carried by the mosquito and is one of the mythical God's creations. The mosquito is uniquely designed. It first injects a fluid into its victim to prevent the victim's blood from coagulating as the blood is withdrawn. Whose side do you think that kind of god is on? We can also consider the West Nile virus, a deadly disease spreading across the United States by the mosquito. As with all other diseases, the mythical creator doesn't offer an antidote, a remedy, or a cure. Humans have to rely on their own intelligence, using methodical, precise scientific procedures to overcome the chaos that exists in the universe. Many have learned and accepted self-reliance to succeed and endure in the chaotic world in which we live. Some people, though, still have the illusion that a messiah will solve their problems.

The common cold, one of many viruses among thousands of diseases at large in our world, should be included as the work of the loving, all-powerful deity if you believe in the creation theory. Believers do not seem to have a problem with this. Nor do believers seem concerned that the divinely inspired authors of the Bible did not mention dietary information about fat, protein, carbohydrates, or the essential mineral elements needed in our diet. Believers are not reminded that the Vatican did not approve of vaccinations until well into the nineteenth century and opposed pain relief for women during childbirth until well into the twentieth century. Christianity's hierarchy believed that suffering is God given. Given that the human body is prone to many defects and the tendency to break down, it would seem, as previously mentioned, that a loving, all-powerful creator would have provided a spare–body parts facility for hearts, lungs, kidneys, knees, hip joints, etc. Fortunately, humans are doing a fairly good job at supplying human body parts and relieving pain without help from the mythical deity.

ASKING FOR FAVORS

❧

Showing favoritism and condoning aggressive behavior as approved by God in the Bible does not result in peaceful, harmonious relationships among friends, neighbors, coworkers, or foreign countries. Since the Bible story has God picking favorites it is now common for athletes to ask God to favor them in sporting activities. If an athlete has some doubt about his or her skill, then asking God for a favor may be worth a try. The Bible set the example with Israelite tribes that lagged far behind the developed world of their time. Suppose an athlete of the opposing team in a competition decides to ask God for the same deal? One athlete is likely to be disappointed; sometimes God seems to ignore both requests. A good coach or a considerate father or friend would gladly offer suggestions to the athlete for improving his or her skills, whereas the athlete's belief in relying on the deity will get no assistance in reinforcing and improving the desired skill. Asking God for favoritism becomes a crutch for doubts of one's ability.

Some hazards are attached to seeking favors from a temperamental, revengeful God, as described in the Bible. For instance, in addition to favoritism, the Bible stories show that God also displays prejudices. In Deuteronomy 20:16–17 God orders the Jews to invade Canaan and kill all Gentiles. The New Testament reports Jesus also had some prejudices. According to Matthew 10:5–6, Jesus is reported to say, "Go not into the way of the Gentiles but rather to the lost sheep of the House of Israel." Unless you are a Jew, asking for favors may come to naught. A careful reading indicates that the God in the Bible belongs to the Jews; therefore Gentiles, Muslims, Hindus, and in fact everyone else should look for their own god.

"Slaughtered" is a word frequently used in the Bible and no doubt is an apt description when war included hand-to-hand combat. It could have been nothing but mayhem, but it pleased God. Modern warfare minimizes the psychological effect that killing may have on soldiers. The modern soldier has to watch TV reports to know his success. The targets in modern warfare are now civilians and the destruction of cities in anticipation that this will cause defenders to call for a cease-fire. What is really incomprehensible is that after thousands of years of war, humans still do not recognize that war and destruction do not produce peace. Wars only create revenge, as is amply demonstrated, beginning with the biblical stories. Humans have been continually led into war by the power structures—namely, the special-interest groups that consist of religion, political power, and those benefiting from military expenditures. Because humans are one of the few animals that kill their own kind, this behavior trait will not be changed or modified except by education. Some so-called developed nations that exist today have only begun to reduce their participation in war, and this can be attributed to their education levels. One stark realization is the economic futility of war, though to date, these "developed" nations are furnishing war materials to anyone, frequently without payment or any real honest hope of ever receiving payment.

Altering the human tendencies toward greed, power, and physical combat will remain an elusive goal. With few exceptions a nation's support for education is not equal to the strength of the entrenched special-interest groups that benefit greatly from war. The preparation for war will continue because the sale or outright gift of military equipment and training is liberally offered by the world's developed nations. Do you recall religion strongly opposing this long continuing cycle of war? "Thou shall not kill" is just pleasing rhetoric, even in the Bible.

THIS IS HARD TO BELIEVE

⌘

Beyond the problems of war, humans continue to believe in biblical stories that are nothing short of kinky. For instance, God insisted that David be treated well. "It came to pass that the Lord smote Nabal that he died" (1 Sam. 25:38). What happens next? David marries Nabal's widow, whom David had been admiring. Now that is a biblical service you may want to keep in mind; God resolves love triangles. David also had a unique way of describing other male persons. In 1 Samuel 25:34 he expresses, "there had not been left unto Nabal any that pisseth against the wall." On the other hand he may have acquired this descriptive language from God, who in 1 Kings 14:10 speaks to Jeroboam's wife saying "I will cut off from Jeroboam him that pisseth against the wall." One can also get the impression that it is best to not mess with God according the message in Zechariah 8:10: "I set all men, everyone against his neighbor." Or, "Behold, I will corrupt your seed, and spread dung upon your faces, even the dung of your solemn feasts" (Mal. 2:3). Or, "And thou shall eat it as barley cakes and thou shall bake it with dung that cometh out of man, in their sight" (Ezek. 4:12). "And thou shalt eat the fruit of thine own body, the flesh of thy sons and daughters which the Lord thy God hath given thee" (Deut. 28:53). Is cannibalism being expressed here? It is doubtful these verses are included in very many religious services or family Bible readings.

Christians, at least clerics, attempt to excuse the crude language and barbaric acts as mysteries performed by their mythical god which humans are not privileged to understand. Because the human memory quickly fades and so few people read the Bible, the fact that the Old Testament does not promise an afterlife is not brought to your attention. Fortunately, the totalitarian despotism that prevailed in the Bible is not condoned in most developed countries today. Only religion and dictators can continue oppressive regimes today. The insecure and those lacking education become victims of sorcerers and charlatans. Because fear is so effective, proof is seldom requested. Only hearsay of an imaginary paradise called heaven seems sufficient for those who are victims of fear.

Custom and tradition are effective deterrents to human thought and behavior, creating a reluctance to challenge the status quo. For this reason, when just starting and struggling to gain new recruits in a new territory, religion absorbed local customs and beliefs, though they were pagan. As a result religious services today include pagan customs and beliefs, like the idea that heaven is upward and hell is downward. Religious services also adopted auditory intonations, perfumery, and claims of transcendental powers common in pagan religions. Although education in developed countries has improved over the last two centuries, including our knowledge of the universe, religion is seldom challenged because of the many unanswered questions about life. Among them, what is the purpose of all life in the universe? An educated, reasoning person is not embarrassed to admit to not knowing all the answers nor frightened by fears offered by religion. Rather, the unknown stimulates many minds to search for answers. This pursuit of knowledge has produced an immense amount of knowledge of the universe, whereas religion continues to promote fear based only on hearsay. Hence, people that look to faith and the help received from lazy minds are willing to follow whatever is popular.

Is it possible that the human mind is more at ease with simple, repetitive dogma? Does self-hypnosis enter into this? At least we know many minds seem willing to accept antiquated religious myths and dogma, though they were created by uneducated, primitive, warring tribal leaders. Perhaps this verifies that ignorance is bliss. Are humans willing to accept the slings and arrows of life, even be banished to some hot place (imaginary and beyond proof, of course) just because a person succumbs to the earthly temptations that abound? Not much comfort can be gained from a Bible that narrows the saved to a select few who can enter the vague and hidden heaven, and a Bible that for centuries ignored slavery and the myriad social problems. Then add to your insecurity the biblical prediction that the wealthy have as much a chance of entering heaven as a camel has of passing through the eye of a needle.

We know from experience that life is grossly unfair. What comfort can the inquiring mind gain from the anti-Gentile bias, made by the Lord in the Old Testament and by Jesus in Matthew 15:24: "I am not sent but unto the lost sheep of the house of Israel"? Or in Matthew 10:5: "Go not into the way of the Gentiles, and into the city of the Samaritans enter ye not." Also in Matthew 10:6: "But go rather to the lost sheep of the house of Israel." In Matthew 15:26 Jesus alludes to Gentiles as dogs. There is another dandy in Luke 8:33, where Jesus casts the devil out of a man and sends the devil into a herd of swine, causing the swine to run violently down a steep place and into a lake where they are choked. The divinely inspired authors have Jesus practicing exorcism. The story does not explain who paid the owner of the swine for his loss. Maybe he was Hebrew and should not have been raising swine, and this was his punishment. If he was a Gentile, then neither the Lord or anyone else seemed to care.

Now, two thousand years later, Jesus' prediction of the Lord appearing to resolve injustice is still on hold. Does it take faith or ignorance to continue to believe? In the meantime, many humans escaped from the Old World's religious oppression and created technical and capital gains beyond the wildest dreams of the ancients. Regardless, people continue to buy Bibles but rarely read them, which gives religion a free hand to embellish descriptions of paradise, though the location is uncertain and the itinerary or agenda for eternity is vague. That is strange, because humans rarely take trips with no idea where they are going or what they will do once they arrive. It is also strange that so many people claim they want to go to heaven yet so few want to die. Could there be some lingering doubt about the place? During the third and fourth centuries the allure of heaven was so oversold that suicides became common as a means of escaping earth's miseries. Religion had to make suicide a no-no. Still this belief in heaven and hell continues because no one returns to refute the myth. Jesus' statement that the Lord would arrive within the lifetime of those hearing him and would determine those to be saved proved to be an illusion.

FOOD AND OTHER MYTHS

∽ʘ∽

An unexplained practice common to early cults and religions was the prohibition of eating certain foods. This was a pagan ritual that religions adopted and which continues to some extent even today. Of course, the people affected by these prohibitions were not consulted; the mandate was a tool of the power structure to increase control and conformity. In a top-down organizational structure a centralized power structure can easily institutionalize dogma, maintain secret documents and files, and establish a self-perpetuating hierarchy that claims to be divinely selected. The dogmas, creeds, canons, rituals, trinkets, and regalia developed by religions do not appear in the Bible but are carryovers from early pagan religions. Catholics opted to forbid eating meat on Friday; Jews selected a command from the Old Testament (Deut. 14:8) that forbids Jews to eat pork because swine do not chew a cud, are unclean, and have divided hooves! Now that is real science. Unfortunately, some of this abracadabra darkness still exists today.

It did not seem to matter that discriminating against pork contradicts religion's own creation story, for the swine in God's creation are innocent of their physical design or eating habits that Jewish religion finds offensive. In India some religions believe the cow is sacred and therefore cannot be eaten. As a result, the cow is allowed to roam at large, dirty the streets, pollute the environment, and endanger the health of the people who elevated the cow to its sacred status. In Alaska early religions made the crow and the raven sacred, and though these birds cause considerable damage and health problems, no one dares to contradict the myths of religion. The early Chinese adopted a custom of ringing a bell to show respect for ancestors. A similar ancient bell ritual exists for the Elevation of the Host during Catholic Mass. The halo adopted by Christians to designate saints is a symbol borrowed from ancient Greeks.

Greek myths were far more imaginative than the myths supporting Christianity. For example the Greek hell had special places of punishment; Tartarus was reserved for notable criminals. Lesser crimes received the punishment of Sisyphus, who was condemned to keep pushing a rock uphill only to find that the rock kept rolling back down. Another novel punishment was invented for Tantalus, who stood in water up to his chin and the water swirled away whenever he tried to drink. The best torture Christians could come up with was fire in the hell they copied from the Greeks. The pictures of hell that Christianity has produced of this imaginary hot place are amazing, but few have asked for proof, so the myth continues to implant fear. Among the list of rituals for inducing conformity are hymns, quivering voices, martial music, and frequent references in the songs and words of Christian soldiers who apparently are exempt from the commandment, "Thou shall not kill." The objective of course is mind control.

MIND CONTROL IS EASY

❧

Actually achieving mind control is not difficult. Cults, totalitarian forms of government, and an assortment of religions successfully use mind control techniques. The most successful create fear, and when applied with dogma and repetitive rote early in the training and development of a human, the success ratio is high. If this methodical, disciplined repetition is maintained, the indoctrinated person will never raise a question about the meaning. In fact, the person can be relied upon to defend it militarily if necessary. For the few individuals who may raise questions about their indoctrination, intimidation remains an effective tool. The so-called tyranny of the masses prevents many people from straying from established convention. How many humans have the courage to stand alone on an issue? You can quickly become an enemy of the masses, and it is safe not to rely upon the masses practicing that biblical suggestion of loving thy enemy or turning the other cheek.

Biblical phrases, somewhat poetic and frequently quoted, are rarely put into practice. Consider the word "peace"; humans have always been allured by the word but have devoted much of their effort and a large portion of their income into preparing for war. This is not surprising given that the Bible is filled with war stories, alleging with pride that tens of thousands of soldiers were involved in various battles. Those who have read the Bible surely recognize that God approved and encouraged wars when he coveted the property of others. Such a role was created for a mythical deity as a cover for the greedy warlords who controlled the remote, backward areas inhabited by Israelites. Today we have advanced far enough to know that the public is unlikely to believe in warlords who have the private ear of a deity. Surprisingly many people still believe in the myths that create religions, until you recognize the insecurity felt by so many people. Religion gives then a security blanket for the adult portion of their life. All believers place God on the winning side in conflicts, and somehow rationalize a loss if one occurs. History and anthropology have observed that in the primitive world the most admired person was the successful warrior. If you wanted to be recognized and honored, you killed people! Generally, this holds true today.

When speaking of the close association of wars and religion it seems appropriate to review Mark Twain's war prayer, particularly since there were more than one hundred wars in various parts of the world during the twentieth century, and no evidence shows that God tried at any time to intervene.

O Lord our God, help us to tear their soldiers to bloody shreds with our shells; help us to cover their smiling fields with the pale forms of their patriot dead; help us to drown the thunder of their guns with shrieks of their wounded, writhing in pain; help to lay waste their humble homes with a hurricane of fire; help us to wring the hearts of their unoffending widows with unavailing grief; help us to turn them out roofless with their little children to wander unfriended the wastes of their desolated land in rags and hunger and thirst, sports of the sun flames of summer and the icy winds of winter, broken in spirit, worn with travail, imploring Thee for the refuge of the grave and denied it—For our sake who adore Thee, Lord blast their hopes, blight their lives, protract their bitter pilgrimage, make heavy their steps, water their way with tears, stain the white snow with the blood of their wounded feet! We ask it in the spirit of love of Him who is the source of love, and who is the ever-faithful refuge and friend of all who are sore of heart and seek His aid with humble and contrite hearts. Amen.

—Mark Twain
The Wit and Wisdom of Mark Twain, Alex Ayres

FEEDING THE SCOURGE

⟶⟵

Since the end of World War II the United States has shipped money, weapons, and soldiers to nearly one hundred nations. We have also trained soldiers of a number of nations. Hot or cold conflicts, the United States continues to participate. Historian Charles Beard describes such action as "perpetual war for perpetual peace, the non-stop conflict that is always justified by the peace just around the corner." Politicians of every stripe keep using the word "peace," apparently because voters like the sound. For some reason, the public does not recognize the inconsistency between the incessant reference to peace and the immense portion of their federal tax money being spent on wars and preparation for wars. If people actually read the Bible, they would recognize it as a history of wars, always conducted with God's approval. Why do humans not recognize the irony, the inconsistency of believing in a deity responsible for creating humans, who are the most destructive and violent of all species? It would help if that loving, all-powerful deity had offered the excuse that he used wars for population control.

However, that would be inconsistent with the biblical reference to be fruitful and populate the earth. This latter reference to reproduction now plagues every nation with economic and social problems, contributes to inequality of opportunity, and is the catalyst for war.

Observing human behavior would lead one to conclude that people prefer to conform rather than face the tyranny of the masses. Conformity makes it easier to get and to hold a job. Conformity is also important if you conduct a business, because religious believers are among those known to boycott a business if the owner or management holds different views. If you do not conform, you even run the chance of being run out of town. The Spanish philosopher Ortega expressed the tyranny of the masses when he said, "The masses crush everything in front of them." For religion to gain mind control over an adult person requires a slightly different approach. This procedure is to exploit the fear of the unknown that resides in many minds since childhood. Pavlov, a psychologist, demonstrated the ease of imposing mind control by routinely ringing a bell at a dog's feeding time. A repetition of this procedure proved the dog would salivate when the bell rang, regardless of whether food was offered. The difference in dealing with humans is that training a dog might be quicker!

Compared to other species, humans find that life's playing field and the rules are different. Most species have the benefit of natural instincts to direct their lives whereas humans possess few instincts other then self-preservation and sex. The fact that humans seem to have a number of emotions that may not exist in other species is perhaps compensation for not being guided by instinct. One powerful reaction exists in all species; it is *fear*, the emotion that overrides all other emotions. What a bonanza the power of fear provides for religions, dictators, and some business practices. If the premise and evidence of your belief or sales pitch is a bit shaky, introducing fear is excellent for circumventing or suppressing the truth. Fear is essential to achieve the brainwashing that allows control. For this reason religion's future has always been quite safe. Without the benefit of instinct humans need to develop and apply reason, but that is an additional mental task the human mind finds hard to apply. Although the human mind can excel in intelligence, the untrained, lazy, and degenerate human mind can behave in a manner that would shame many animals.

When the minds of the young are programmed almost from birth with the fear projected by religion, along with superstition and misinformation held by some parents, plus peer pressure encountered while growing up, the chance for a reasoning, logically thinking individual can be quite remote. For example note the increase in the number of cults (estimated at around seven hundred) that exist just in the United States and the control that religion has gained over politicians and political parties since the 1960s. The beginning of this decline in reason and logic coincides with the U.S. engagement in a very unpopular war in Vietnam. During the turbulent 1960s the young people's protests were met by timid educators. Student sit-ins were able to achieve revisions of curriculums to relevant subjects as determined by the students. The ensuing turmoil opened the door for the federal government's intervention into education, resulting in a precipitous decline of SAT scores and the rapid escalation in the cost of education.

As the level of education and knowledge declined, the vacuum was filled by myths and faith offered by religion. A current evaluation compares well with history; when education levels are lowest, religion has its greatest strength. This climate also allows religion to gain a foothold in government, giving some, though not all, religions access to public funding. Government, of course, is a power structure that frequently abuses the democratic principle of equity and fairness to all. Historically, the collusion of religion and government has not been in religion's best interest. Unfortunately, people show little interest in history; the concern is for the immediate, the short term, rather than analyzing long-term results. History also shows that when religions and governments are in collusion, religion becomes a partner in the abuse of power and corruption. Why does this happen? The dominant drives in humans are power and greed, which are capable of overriding any interest in history. Humans have a record of repeating their mistakes, making progress very slow. Again, this human failure is well described by author George Santayana: "Those who cannot remember the past are condemned to repeat it."

Dumbing Down Makes a Path

❦

The dumbing down of America has occurred over the past four decades, as federal largess inflates the public debt. The national government engages in questionable accounting to offset its profligate spending by dipping into Social Security funds to camouflage the real public debt. Every local, county, and state government and quasi-government activity has become dependent upon federal funding as politicians respond to the public whims and organized pressure groups. It does not occur to the general public that the government has no money until it takes the public's money in taxes. When tax revenues do not cover the government's spending, Congress merely adds to the public debt without consulting the public. The total debt then keeps compounding, deferring it to future generations. A surreptitious concentration of federal power is easily achieved when public knowledge is declining. The sum total of the debt grows beyond comprehension, and apathy ensues. As a reward for their derelict action the public has given political office-holders virtually lifetime positions. Ninety-eight percent of incumbents were returned to office in the election of 2000, a percentage higher than in the Russian legislature, the Duma. Politicians quickly learn to take credit for the rabbit-in-the-hat trick without even blushing as they congratulate themselves for returning a reduced portion of the public's own money in the form of federal grants. The public no longer questions the system, appearing mesmerized in the belief that elected officials know how to spend the public's money better than the individual taxpayer could. A new form of utopia evolved as personal responsibility became passé; people replaced responsibility with the concept of rights to almost everything. Humans are the only species that believe someone else is responsible for their support. Because religion is among the beneficiaries of profligate government spending, no protests are heard from the pulpit.

Though lacking the benefits of instinct, the human brain supposedly is provided a more valuable attribute through the ability to reason. To date the reasoning ability of humans is either grossly underused or possibly underdeveloped. Certainly the brain does not automatically slip into a reasoning mode when confronted with a problem or when faced with the task of sorting out facts before making a decision. Unfortunately the human mind requires many years, estimated to be at least into a person's early twenties, before reaching the capability of mature reasoning. Even then we have no guarantee that reasoning will take place unless a concerted and developed practice of evaluating the available information takes place. As a result, human progress on social and economic matters is extremely slow. Custom and tradition add a further drag to employing logic and reason. Add to those impediments to reasoning how a person's home, school, and religion impact the mind during the first twenty years of a person's life. The impact upon the mind during those early development years can virtually remove the courage to break with tradition. Hence conformity and the status quo prevail, causing change and human progress to take decades, even centuries to occur.

In addition to the inhibiting factors to the reasoning process noted above, humans may have an obstacle posed by an ego. The ancient patriarchs who guarded and directed the stories of Israel's myth of being God's favorites may have allowed ego to rationalize the murder, genocide, rape, incest, and aggravated assault that is found in Old Testament stories. Claiming humans to be a superior species is an attempt to whitewash the cruelty and indecencies recorded in the Bible. With the aid of archaeology some of these sordid biblical stories show discrepancies in time, location, and the characters involved. Unless a reader has been indoctrinated to believe without questioning the biblical stories of God commanding the annihilation of entire communities and approving slavery and the abuse of women and children, an educated person cannot accept the biblical authors as divinely inspired. What purpose could possibly have been in mind to produce a story of unbelievable violence and deviant behavior? What is really amazing is the wide acceptance of these myths by otherwise knowledgeable people in the twenty-first century. For example, Exodus 35:2 states that those who work on Sunday shall be put to death. Leviticus 25:44 deals with buying slaves. In Judges 1:1–4 the Lord sends Judah to take over the Canaanites, and Judah slays ten thousand men. Almost from the beginning, Abraham fakes conversations with the Lord to justify trying to take all the land from the Nile to the Euphrates River. Even more amazing to believe is that this myth is justification for the present-day taking of land by Israelis. It is a mystery that religion is allowed such errors in judgment and interpretation of justice by nations considered to be educated.

THE BIBLE AS A GUIDE

❦

Believers in the Judeo-Christian tradition claim that the Bible provides solutions to world problems, but is the father figure in the Bible one to emulate? The legal system in developed nations today would find God guilty of child abuse and mass murder. The sole purpose and intent of the biblical stories, claiming to be divinely inspired, is to require conformity, submission, and sacrifices, and to permit Israelite warriors, declared as God's favorites, to invade, take land and possessions, and enslave the victims. The penalty for violating any of the first seven commandments is death. In Iran, Iraq, the Sudan, and Afghanistan religion dominates government, and God does not intervene to reduce oppression and murder if the carnage is carried out in the name of religion.

Imagine the progress humans would have achieved if the divinely inspired authors of the Bible had included the periodic table of chemical elements and given a few hints on locating and extracting Earth's resources. It would be hard to find human parents who would withhold knowledge valuable to their children. How is one to be guided through the bit about human sacrifices? The hierarchy's power structure justified this carnage as necessary to please the Lord. When looking for guidance, it should be remembered that the long, painful history of the human struggle to escape oppression and to establish a judicial system to protect individual rights and freedom was not gracefully granted by religion. Religions did not object and bring an end to the Salem witch trials in this country, which resulted in the execution of twenty innocent people based solely on hysteria and hearsay. One hundred fifty others were falsely imprisoned during that reign of terror. Some confessed under torture to such fantasies as flying through the air or partaking of witch sacraments. It was a judge who finally brought the killing to an end by refusing to accept hearsay to convict people. Pope Gregory in the thirteenth century set a precedent for this hysteria by authorizing the killing of witches. In 1484 Pope Innocent VIII issued a bull declaring witches a reality, and to doubt this declaration was heresy.

The fragility of the human brain leaves the door wide open for manipulation by power structures that design a step-by-step plan to gain control of a person's thoughts. On the brighter side, if you are considering various fields of employment, counseling may have potential. Today almost any tragedy or upsetting incident seems to call for counselors. Of course, religion snaps to attention when tragedies occur, quickly calling for prayers, because someone may ask why God allowed the tragedy to happen in the first place. Of course, any call for prayer can count on politicians and public officials making a pious appearance. After all, the main objective of an elective officeholder is to be reelected. Never mind that Jesus is quoted in the Bible as saying those who pray in public are hypocrites, or that not one command in all of the Gospels supports public prayer. Of course the politicians like many voters are not familiar with the Bible they claim to be their guide on all matters.

Humans are inclined to accept a religious belief without questioning whether it can be proven or requires blind faith. Why such indifference? A good guess is it takes much less time and thought to accept rather than question and try to verify. Also, religion is largely inherited, and by the time one is prepared to question a belief, time and personal courage become factors.

Modern scholars of Christianity conclude that the Gospels as they appear in the Bible were completed after the destruction of the Jewish Temple, approximately 70–72 C.E., or almost forty years after the death of Jesus. Historians of theology, including a study by the Oxford University Society of Historical Theology, conclude that no evidence of the Gospels existed before the end of the first century. This long delay may explain why the Gospel of Mark does not even mention the birth of Jesus. Matthew and Luke were probably written in the last decade of the first century. The first mention of Jesus' birth was at least ninety years after the event, indicating that the alleged deity did not consider the event important and made no arrangements for documenting the event. During the second century the Christian religion, which at the time probably had the status of a cult, had to compete with Greek, Persian, Jewish, and Egyptian cults, as well as mystics. These contemporaries influenced the development of Christianity, including its adoption of some of the beliefs and practices of existing, pagan religions. The delay in writing the Gospels of the New Testament explains why several are listed as "The Gospel According To," indicating it was not written by the named "author." No central authority was responsible for preparing the New Testament. Hence the final draft occurred after sorting out a large number of writings.

One thing is perfectly clear; two thousand years after Jesus is quoted as saying "the end is near," his prediction was like dozens of other predictions—about as accurate as a weather forecast. Instead, life with all its brutality and oppression went on as usual. Humans muddled through the Dark Ages, the Crusades, and the Spanish Inquisition conducted by Christian clerics, but fortunately rare, brave individuals continued the struggle to gain freedom and resisted the oppression of religion and government. What an indictment on the human species and its religions—that millions of people still lack personal freedom and are oppressed by totalitarian power structures.

After a long period of increased resistance, clerics were forced to modernize, even adopt PR methods to improve the image of religion. Dress codes in church were relaxed and flextime for worship introduced. Biblical passages are carefully selected to omit the obscenities and the violence. Passages that criticize accumulated wealth and worldly goods are omitted; if you recall, Jesus did not have much hope for the rich. Some Catholic bishops have even recommended that the Vatican drop offending passages from the church's official reading list. Passages by both St. Paul and St. Peter that offend and demean women are usually deleted from Scripture readings. The latter may not apply to those Baptists who cling to the belief that wives must be submissive. Reluctance to change by the Vatican's power structure still persists for fear of endangering the infallibility edict and the creation myth.

Why has it taken so long to reach our current level of intelligence? For some fifteen hundred years beyond the New Testament stories, religion stonewalled education. The self-appointed clerics were ignorant, but they knew enough to deny the public access to learning that would elevate the public above the cleric's intelligence. Even St. Paul maintained that interpreting the Bible was the exclusive right of the clergy.

(Rom. 13:6, 15:16; Heb. 7:20-21; 1Tim. 2:12) Clerics feared an informed public.

The discovery of isolated cells other than ones found in embryos by researchers in Karolinska Institute in Stockholm demonstrates the value of unfettered, unbiased science. Their discovery is the capability of different cell types to divide and transform when the need arises. This raises the prospect of regenerative medicine. However, when religion dominates government to the point that President Bush stops stem cell research, this appears to be a return of religion's restriction on knowledge that prevailed for centuries. In such a climate, scientific research in the United States will fall behind other developed nations, even behind some emerging nations.

Reality tells us that a rough world exists out there with unforgiving physical laws and carnivorous creatures that survive by eating each other. It is not a pretty sight to observe a beautiful songbird eaten alive, torn apart bit by bit by a sparrow hawk that also happens to be one of the mythical deity's creatures. Man himself does not kill just to eat as other animals do. The human creature, created according to the myth in the image of God, kills to eat, kills for sport, and is one of the few species that kills his own kind. In fact humans have killed until they have wiped out some species. The ambiguity of the Bible is apparent to any scholar of the book as well as to many educated persons. Surveys show that the nonbeliever is often the better educated. Only children, the opinionated, the zealots, or the fanatics are unconcerned with the ambiguity of the Bible.

FAITH VS. REASON

❧

Ironically, natural disasters are often called acts of God. It would be difficult to find a normal human so fiendish as to drown everyone except one family. The mythical God did, without objection from believers; read Genesis 6:7. This watery grave included infants and children, though it is hard to imagine them as guilty of the evil acts that displeased this Creator. Can you picture parents with their small children and infants, clinging to trees but finally drowning, as the loving, all-powerful, all-knowing God gloats in revenge? There may be some consolation to discover that archaeologists consider this an exaggerated tale, like the many fabricated myths in the Bible. The biblical flood is not mentioned in any other historical source. The only fragment of credibility to the biblical flood is that archaeologists have found buried sand deposits along sections of the Euphrates River, indicating flooding occurred in a limited area at some point in time. For people living thousands of years ago to believe that biblical tale is understandable; that it is believed today can only be the result of brainwashing and a power structure's use of fear.

Had the early residents of the Euphrates River area known the world included mountains more than twenty thousand feet high they might have modified their stories a bit. In his day a vivid imagination and the freedom to exaggerate would enhance a storyteller's reputation. It also helps to recognize the Israelite patriarchs conjuring this story were at one time captives of the Babylonians and undoubtedly heard the myths and tales of that area. Years later as the Israelites made up their own creation myth they included the myths of organized ignorance of that time period. We should be willing to excuse those misinformed storytellers, but what can be said for people who today believe the stories are divinely inspired? Recently a Texas mother drowned her five children and the law did not give her a reprieve; she is in prison. Her defense attorney did not try to compare her action with that of a disgruntled God who wiped out all but one family. If only one family was left, the storytellers didn't know the effect of incest and inbreeding. How many people searching their roots want to believe their ancestry began with incest in Noah's family?

Once in a while you hear someone describe multiple births as a miracle or an act of God. A reasoning person recognizes that the woman's normal reproductive process was defective and that fertility pills, a scientific development, were employed. When the multiple babies arrive, they may require mechanical incubators, also the work of science. Many multiple birth babies would not survive without the help of science. Believers are inclined to give God credit for a miracle when someone recovers from an illness or escapes with their life in an accident, even though this same God ignores or overlooks thousands of very nice people, including babies, suffering from illnesses, from which they do not recover. If prayer improves the survival rate, then religious hospitals adorned with icons and crosses should have a lower mortality rate than nonreligious hospitals. That statistic seems to be missing. Fortunately for mystics, charlatans, and deceivers who claim to perform miracles, the human body has great restorative power and overcomes many illnesses. Those who claim to have healing powers are not about to walk through a hospital to demonstrate that power.

The human inclination toward violence is a factor in the rapid increase in the U.S. prison population, which happens to be four times higher in proportion to our population than in any other advanced civilized nation. However, some comfort may be found in knowing most of our prisoners consider themselves as believers in religion! A big factor in this increase in our prison population is our drug problem. Why would a loving God create all these mind-altering plants and the desire in humans to use them? Do you know of any other species with a drug problem? Of course, no other species is considered important enough to get the stamp of being created in the image of God. When the early warlords claimed humans were made in the image of God, did it mean God was a drug user too?

The Bible does not appear among the list of books people are reading, published frequently in magazines and newspapers. The leaders of Judaism and Christianity should be pleased, because if people took the time to read the Bible, many more would be turned off. Next question: why do Bible sales remain high? Do people feel that if you place the Bible on a table, particularly where people see it, friends and relatives will be impressed? Is that being honest? Are ethics being stretched? Or do they believe that by walking past the Bible an osmotic effect or absorption will take place? In the latter case, some care and thought is recommended on where to locate the Bible. Some undesirable human characteristics such as revenge are attributed to God and frequently mentioned in the Bible. For example check Nahum 1:2: "[T]he Lord revengeth and is furious. The Lord will take vengeance on his adversaries, and He reserveth wrath for His enemies." Does it please you that this bit about loving one's enemies, or loving thy neighbor, as set forth in the Old Testament, can be revoked at opportune times? This bit of Scripture may be the origin of the expression, "Don't get mad, get even!" The Bible includes some examples of human compassion, but all religions as far back as can be traced recognized the importance of compassion and love. Even animal species display caring actions.

WHERE IS GOD WHEN NEEDED?

❦

Pol Pot, the Khmer Rouge leader from 1975 to 1979, is judged as responsible for killing an estimated 1.6 million to 2 million Cambodian men, women, and children. Another tragic event occurred near the end of World War I; the outbreak of Spanish flu spread worldwide, killing more than 20 million people. This epidemic stimulated interest in research of viral infections, ultimately leading to the knowledge of cell structure, DNA, and the body's immune system. Again, the knowledge of science provided the wellspring for human progress, whereas religion for centuries acted as a brake on acquiring knowledge. Or take the worst single weather calamity, Hurricane Mitch, which killed some 11,000 people in Central America and an undetermined number of animals. Honduras suffered the most loss of life, and the property damage will require decades to restore. In spite of prayers, no advance message was ever received from the mythical deity or assistance given in the reconstruction.

Many times in human history, individuals like Idi Amin of Uganda and other rogues have made life painful, even hideous. The mythical God did not interfere in the genocide Amin committed and now allows him to spend his remaining years comfortably in the safety of an Arabic country. Joseph Stalin is credited with eliminating an estimated 30-40 million lives through the Gulag, murder, and forced collectivization of farms, yet he lived to a ripe old age. The infamous Adolf Hitler murdered 6 million or more Jews as he endeavored to build a super race. Hitler was able to tilt the scale of justice severely with the help he received from surprising quarters. After the burning of the German Reichstad and Hitler's rise to power, Pope Pius XII was among the first to give diplomatic recognition to Hitler's Third Reich, a recognition that was never withdrawn.

The fascist Ustashas party in Croatia became part of Hitler's war machine, assisting in locating Jews and sending them to concentration camps during World War II. The wealth of the victims, amounting to billions of dollars, has been traced to banks in several so-called neutral countries. These banks recently opened their archives and bank records to assist in the search for the stolen wealth. Because of the Vatican's financial dealings with the Nazis and their allies, and the aid given by Croatian Catholic priests to help Croatian war criminals escape to South America, questions were raised regarding the Vatican's knowledge of the laundered funds. The Vatican refused investigators access to its archives despite requests from several nations and Jewish groups. Why do believers allow their religions to act as secret societies? Is the power structure afraid that examination will find the basis of its dogma misleading or that its wealth will become public?

A comprehensive view of events in the universe indicates a continually changing, random chaos, producing atmospheric and firmament eruptions that destroy property and kill and injure many people. A reasonable person could logically ask, what or where is the guidance for this complex system? Or what is key to the sources of energy, including the biological, electrochemical, precise mathematical force or law, of which to date science has discovered only bits and pieces? As late as the time of Columbus, belief in a flat world was common. Columbus and a few other pioneers believed the world was round and therefore they could sail around it. For progress to occur, one needs to remember Will Rogers's homespun explanation, "Ignorance is not the problem. It is what we know that ain't so that is the problem."

Our knowledge of the universe is very recent, most of it discovered during the twentieth century, and we recognize that much more is waiting to be learned. For example, the Milky Way galaxy that includes Earth is one hundred thousand light years wide, one thousand light years thick, and filled with a few hundred billion stars. You won't find this in the Bible. Stars form or are born; older stars explode and fade away. Astronomers believe that at the center of our galaxy is a black hole, the description of an area so dense that nothing, not even light, can escape from its gravitational pull. That is not in Genesis. For millennia religion denied humans the freedom to explore science and gain the knowledge to reduce drudgery and ill health. The human mind had to be freed of the myths and fear imposed by religion to attain the intelligence and lifestyle present today.

We now know that the objects in our galaxy orbit the galactic center. The size of the galaxy is so immense that light from a star at one edge takes one hundred thousand years to reach the opposite side of the galaxy, though one light year equals 6 trillion miles. A recently discovered galaxy named the Whirlpool is positioned 35 million light years from Earth. A group of some thirty galaxies, including our own, stretch in numerous directions beyond the Milky Way, and extend some 4 million light years across. The two largest galaxies in the group are the Milky Way and the Andromeda galaxy. Though Andromeda is 2 million light years from Earth, it can be seen from Earth with the naked eye. The early humans on Earth knew only of the beauty of the sky and compared its beauty to the difficulties they experienced on Earth. Quite naturally, they imagined that somewhere in the beauty of the sky there would be a place of comfort and peace, a relief from the grim, often violent life on Earth. The mythmakers, represented by the power structure, used the dream created by the sky to capitalize on human ignorance. It was a sure thing, because if anyone questioned the myth, they were charged with blasphemy that was punishable by death. The mythical deity did not interfere. Give the power structure credit: it worked then and continues to fool many today.

AESOP'S FABLE FOR ADULTS

❦

Aesop was the author of children's fables and lived around the sixth century B.C. He is credited as a valuable teacher of ethics and morality in a period when these characteristics and knowledge of any sort was scarce. The mythical deity left only commands. Parents of children in those early days believed Aesop's fables were a great help in caring for and instructing children, as most adults lacked knowledge in child rearing. So important was survival that people often resorted to animal instincts to plunder and kill. Myths filled the black hole of ignorance; the clever, zealous individuals could become story-tellers, even claim the ability to communicate with spirits. Today it is hard to believe that anyone privileged in the educational system in a developed nation would not apply reason and recognize the biblical stories of creation in Genesis as a myth or fairy story that suited ignorant masses. As illogical as the biblical myths seem, they continue because many have heard them since childhood. While growing up, one quickly learns that accepting the tyranny of the masses is safer than expressing doubt. Unfortunately, humans are often influenced by the tyranny of the masses that results in abusing people with different ideas.

Some of the biblical inconsistencies with common morality, such as murder, rape, and incest, have already been noted. Starting with Genesis we are told that God created man in his own image and that God saw everything and "Behold it was very good." Then with no explanation regarding the source of material, God forms on Earth every beast and fowl and brings them to Adam to see what he would call them. We read that "whatsoever Adam called every living creature, that was the name thereof." Now Adam had to be one sharp dude, because he had hundreds of thousands to name. Because God did not think to create writing, all of Adam's work was in vain. Millions of years later, in 1763, Carl Linnaeus created the first uniform system of naming genera and species, establishing a global system of naming life forms.

If we exclude the extinct species, such as dinosaurs, that the Bible and Noah do not even mention, an estimated fifty thousand vertebrates, 30 million invertebrates, and 100 million different insects live on Earth. As noted earlier, no mention is made of the germs, viruses, and pathogens, and believers would rather not credit these to God. Scientists believe at least 1 million species of fungus, some good and some bad, exist, and these have not been mentioned in creation or the effect these living creatures have on health, plus the damage done to agriculture.

On the third day of the creation myth, God's attention turned to plants, grass, herbs, and fruit trees. Botanical records show some 500,000 types of plants. Within the types also many species exist; for example, 230 different species of rhododendrons have been identified in China. More than 20,000 varieties of orchids also exist. Based on the Genesis story God deserves an award for productivity. Counting just the known plant species, omitting the new ones that continue to be discovered, God would have created plants at the rate of 347 species per minute, or 5.8 plants per second. He does even better on creatures. Take just the vertebrates, invertebrates, and insects, a total of 130,050,000, and his productivity rate increases to 1505 creatures per second. This does not include the germs, viruses, and pathogens that biblical authors omitted. Also the exact number of fish and sea creatures is unknown, as scientists continue to discover new aquatic creatures. The number of species is really astounding. Among the beetles, 350,000 have been identified. Millions more are probably still to be discovered in tropical rain forests around the world. Unfortunately, Adam was not given the ability to write. Any proof would have removed religion from its status of being hearsay. Of course, though, God probably had much on his mind.

Genesis doesn't mention the complexity of the molecular structure of DNA, a part of all species. The alleged loving deity did not mention DNA in the Bible, though its recent discovery is vital to human health. This discovery and the subsequent genome studies have opened up amazing data. Think of the advances that will be made with the discovery of the four nucleotides, identified as A, C, T, and G that make up a gene, the order of which determines traits. For example 70 percent of the genes of the *C. elegans,* a one-millimeter-long worm, a nematode found in soil, and among the first to have its DNA disentangled, has the same genes found in the human body. Plant breeding, selection plus crossbreeding, can attain larger, sweeter varieties. The wild tomato was transformed from marble sized to the large size currently raised. Likewise, corn has been improved from being virtually grass to large production levels. With biotechnology, plants may offer a substitute for the pesticides and herbicides used extensively in agriculture today, which will bring benefits to the health of humans and animals.

Why would this knowledge have been withheld by a loving, all-powerful deity? Of course, the intent of the biblical story was for God's favorite people, the backward Israelite tribes, to justify wars to acquire the land and wealth of others. It's a ruse, but many believe it. The promoters of Christianity and all other religions depend on hearsay. Why does it work? Because the fear of death and punishment is instilled early in life, and many people are willing to buy it.

The research into the human genome, the chromosomes of organisms, is expected to lead to treatments for disorders like Alzheimer, Hodgkin's disease, diabetes, schizophrenia, and cancer, as well as diseases like the plague, smallpox, and yellow fever. At times diseases have decimated large portions of the world population. Of course, no disease preventative is mentioned in the Bible. Its only purpose was to establish a power structure for control and for humans to continue to submit to myths and superstitions. Modern parents who withheld such vital health information from their children would not only be severely criticized but would likely be charged with the crime of parental neglect.

In the biblical story God is credited with creating the stars but plays it safe by not explaining their distance from Earth, why they emit light or how many may exist. Astronomers had to discover these details. Early humans believed the stars were close to Earth. Centuries passed until men like Bruno, Galileo, and Copernicus confronted the ignorance that religion supported, and of course these pioneers were dealt with severely by religion's hierarchy. Current estimates holds that billions of stars and possibly billions of galaxies exist, of which Earth represents just a small part of one of the galaxies. Genesis credits God with creating the heavens on the third day. To create just one billion stars in a day would require making more than 11,500 per second. Of course, fairy tales and myths are not restricted to facts.

The Bible credits God with making land, though the details of procuring the ingredients are scant. The Bible doesn't mention whether God left the land in just one glob or shaped the continents and positioned them on the planet. The Bible states that the planet was flat, and this error prevailed even to the time of Columbus. When minds are controlled by myths, very little progress ever occurs. The story does not mention that Earth consists of tectonic plates or that landmasses drift, and that changes in the tectonic plates cause earthquakes. We now know that geologically Earth required millions of years to form. The strata of various rock, soil, and lava are plainly visible to the eye of any observer. Ancient creatures, big and small, are also imbedded in the strata, proving the time required to form Earth is far greater than the Bible's genealogical calculation of Earth's age at less than six thousand years. We have adequate proof that Earth is several billion years old.

In Genesis 1:31, "God saw everything and it was good." God's opinion of his own work ends quickly. By Genesis 6:7, he has already changed his mind, saying, "I will destroy man whom I have created, from the face of the Earth; both man and beast, and the creeping things and the fowl of the air for it repenteth me that I have made them." The Bible doesn't say whether in his limitless power he tried to correct any errors. It appears he had temper tantrums. Whatever happened to compassion and love? Also, how do animals or insects, the creeping things and the fowl, sin in the eyes of the deity? Is this an early example of Lord Acton's expression, "Power tends to corrupt and absolute power corrupts absolutely"? A reasoning, thinking mind would immediately recognize this as a fairy tale.

The next move in this fable is God's selection of a family of eight, four males and four females, to be survivors. The fairy tale continues with the deity destroying everything except Noah, his wife, and three sons, Shem, Ham, and Japheth, and their wives. Note again, the patriarchs that dreamed up this story do not consider women important enough to mention names. A reasoning mind that actually takes the time to read this would conclude it lacks the essentials of being even a mediocre fairy story. Of the more than 100 million creatures on Earth, Noah is instructed to collect two of everything (that doubles the total!) along with food for the trip.

God instructs Noah to make the boat 300 cubits long, 50 cubits wide and 30 cubits high. The cubit is an ancient unit of measure, the distance from the middle finger to the elbow, varying from 18 to 22 inches. Giving the benefit of the doubt and using a 22-inch measurement, the boat would be 549 feet long, 91.5 feet wide, and 55 feet high. By God's instructions the boat was to have one window and a door and be three stories high. One window and one door, even if liberally construed to be for each floor of the deck, would result in some stench from all the animal dung. (No EPA existed, so the dung could be thrown overboard.) Can you imagine the job of cleaning three floors of a floating five-hundred-foot barnyard with only one door and one window per floor? Consider the logistics for providing and storing enough food for forty days, plus separating millions of creatures, many that normally eat each other. How much hay would be required for just a pair of elephants? Actually there would be four elephants, the African species and the Indian elephant species. Where would Noah have stored enough for thousands of species for forty days? Even a fairy story should not leave so many loose ends. It is curious that biblical stories seem obsessed with the number 40. The patriarch's stories have Moses on the Mount talking to God for forty days and wandering around in the desert with his band of followers for forty years.)

What a shame Noah's ship log was not preserved to tell an even longer tale of how he gathered all the animals and insects?

Some animals are carnivores. Without refrigeration, how did Noah keep a meat supply, or did he load some extra animals to be killed for meat? The interior of that boat gets messier with every thought or question raised. To substantiate this tale, Noah had to collect animals from all over the globe, and most animals are fierce critters. How did he capture the American buffalo when America had not been discovered until 1492? Did Noah get to America before Columbus? Getting the rare species from Australia and the Galapagos Islands, the penguins in Antarctica, and the Arctic polar bears would make the story very interesting. How did Noah gather and hold these critters until all, thousands of them, were captured and ready to be loaded? Maybe it is not worth worrying about, because many people readily accept and believe the story whether it makes sense or not. Religion comes off better if one does not think too deeply about the stories.

Noah was 600 years old, (Gen. 8:16) was he a senior citizen? The depth of water reached 15 cubits, (Gen. 8:20) or about 28 feet. There are mountains on Earth that exceed 20,000 feet. There appears to be a problem! The Ark rested in the seventh month, which could be August, but we don't know when the trip started, so we have to admit things are a bit fuzzy. To add to this quandary, Genesis 8:5 states: "Waters decreased continually until the tenth month when the tops of the mountains were seen." Later Genesis says Noah sent a dove out and the dove returned, and Noah concluded that no land was visible. Later a second dove is released and it does not return, so Noah concludes that land is visible somewhere. Finally in Genesis, God spoke to Noah telling him to unload the ark. Nothing is said about how Noah got all these animals back to where they came from. Did Noah just open the one door on each level of the boat and shoo the animals out to fend as best they could on barren land? Of course, no laws on cruelty to animals had been written yet.

Do you recall that famous baseball quote, "It ain't over 'til its over"? The Bible states Noah was 601 years old when he completed the trip, and that he lived 350 years afterwards. It takes a really dedicated believer to gloss over stories with such exaggerations. Modern scientists estimate that if all the ice on our planet melted, the ocean levels would increase about five feet. The Bible story has the water level covering mountains that we know are over twenty thousand feet high. Other major problems should be considered; any herdsman recognizes the danger of reducing the number in any species to two creatures. The reason is the possibility of disease killing them when confined to small, poorly ventilated, and unclean quarters. How did Noah capture and preserve insects and bacteria, or did God create new species after unloading the ark? Most people who have grown plants would recognize that the soil condition would be badly leached and infertile.

What might be the reason for the divinely inspired authors of the Bible to spin such a tall tale? At one time in early history the Israelites were held as slaves in the area described as flooded. In recent decades archaeological digs have found evidence of large sand deposits adjacent to the Euphrates River, indicating a flood of some size probably occurred at some time in history. In ancient times, including when the Old Testament stories were being told and passed along, people had no idea of the size of the world. If at one time early people could only see water, their world may have seemed flooded. Again, you have a story passed along by patriarchs but one that is not recorded in any other piece of history.

The continuation of this story recites some degrading social patterns that apparently suited the ancient patriarchs who devised the mythical God. After the flood, and for no explained reason, Noah imposed the name Canaan on his son Ham. Possibly this was to ridicule and lay the groundwork for subsequent moves by Israel to degrade residents of Canaan. The Bible's alleged invasion of Canaan is not supported by archaeological evidence that has since been uncovered. The one consistent thread running through all the biblical stories covering millennia is the justification of invasions and acquisition of land by Israel. It amounts to patriarchs fabricating stories of Israel's history, but that is not documented by any other historical source.

The biblical story continues with Noah planting a vineyard after the flood. We are not told how long it took to get a crop of grapes, only that he made wine and got drunk. (He probably needed to forget the boat and the animals!) Contrary to the story being family reading material, Noah gets drunk and while lying in a drunken stupor in a tent, his son Ham observes his naked father and lays a cover over him. When Noah sobers up he curses Ham, and begins to refer to Ham as Canaan. Keep in mind these are God's esteemed, hand-picked humans for reestablishing a just and admirable human species, which would repopulate the world after God sterilized and sanitized the world with a flood to rid it of riff-raff characters. Noah further degrades his son Ham by condemning him to be a servant to the other brothers. This may offer some enlightenment on why the human race continues to have many societal problems. Do you want to believe that your ancestry is traceable to Noah? Of course, the patriarch storytellers created their own history, keeping a power structure intact and manipulating stories of a mythical deity to fit their goal of land acquisition. The flood story set the stage for later episodes in the biblical myths of Israelite warriors receiving God's instructions to wage war on Canaan.

ANOTHER REVELATION

～○～

Does it seem strange that the background of people who start religions is always obscure? In the sixth century, around 570, an Arab named Mohammed was born in Mecca. Orphaned at around age six and raised by an uncle, he became a camel driver in a trading center visited by many caravans. Mecca was also the center of the Kaaba religion, where a black stone believed to have magical powers attracted many pilgrims from all over Arabia. Animism was a common belief, but local tribes also created various deities. Slavery was common to all religions, and slaves were acquired by plunder and raids, a common means of gaining wealth. All deities were maintained by power structures, and all approved of slavery. As an adult, Mohammed prospered in the commercial life of the area. He married a wealthy woman and sired several children.

At around age forty Mohammed claimed he had a revelation. Like Jesus, Mohammed could neither read nor write, so the Qur'an was written by people with a vested interest, the power structure, after Mohammed's death. Like the Bible the

246 • Beware of Talking Snakes

Qur'an consists of commands. The revelations that Mohammed
is alleged to have experienced claimed to be from the angel
Gabriel as well as directly from God. Mohammed lived about
twenty years after his first revelation. Because Mohammed was
illiterate, the revelations were passed along orally to others who
claim to have learned the revelations. This too is similar to the
New Testament stories that were written by others, claiming to
repeat the words of Jesus, as they were divinely inspired. After
Mohammed's death those claiming to have learned the revelations put them together in what is called the Qur'an, meaning
"recitation." It is estimated the Qur'an was completed about
twenty years after Mohammed's death. One of Mohammed's
wives, Aisha, provided orally 1,210 messages of the Qur'an she
claimed Mohammed expressed to her. Now that has to be a
photographic mind. The earliest biographies about Mohammed
were done an estimated 120 to 200 years after his death and also
cite miraculous events that cannot be proven. Religions require
a lot of faith.

Information on Mohammed's life is scant. Some oral
reports indicate he exhibited an unsettled mental state, with
revelations received during hallucinations. Defenders describe
him as falling into a faint, sweating, and trembling. Mohammed
apparently expressed or described his revelations to persons
around him. Some claimed to have learned the revelations and
recited them to others, though various personal expressions by
those repeating the revelation could have been inserted into the
Qur'an.

During Mohammed's business life he dealt with caravans,
which exposed him to knowledge of the outside world. It is
possible that he became convinced of the hopelessness of his
own people, who were mired in idolatry and superstition.
Though severely limited by circumstance he may have felt
obligated to try to bring some enlightenment. Monotheism

most likely had filtered in from the outside world, and it may have seemed an improvement in a world that for most people had no explanation. In what seems to be somewhat a tormented life, Mohammed appointed himself as a prophet of God. He believed something was responsible for the world, and in an effort to advance his own people, he copied from other religions, including the beliefs about judgment after death, resurrection, charity, fasting, and obedience.

Typically the promotion of new ideas always meets resistance. For Mohammed the traditionalists felt threatened and angry, and criticism increased. He received threats, prompting him to move from Mecca to Medina, where his beliefs found acceptance. It is also quite typical for zealots to become adamant in their beliefs, and Mohammed was no exception. He began to assemble an army, also typical for religions. With an army to back him, Mohammed changed from merely offering revelations to issuing commands. He had a power structure, and the combination of church and state took form. The mosque and state became the foundations of Islam. This idea would not have been new to Mohammed, for Constantine combined church and state in the fourth century, transforming the Bible into an ideological weapon. The combination sanctified the use of force when moral virtues were not enough. The financial support needed for Islam's military arm came from raiding bands, particularly raids on caravans that had been Mohammed's business life.

Mohammed's theological views are patterned after the Old Testament. During his working life he became familiar with Israeli customs and beliefs. He adopted monotheism, observed Yom Kippur, and faced Jerusalem to pray. When he learned the Israelites had rejected Christianity, he turned prayers toward Mecca instead of Jerusalem. In May 627, Mohammed's army massacred an Israelite tribe, decapitating men, women, and children, and divided up the livestock. Moses, Joshua, and Gideon, to mention just a few of Old Testament heroes, also massacred their opponents. Later as Mohammed's military victories expanded his control, he permitted Jewish residents to keep their property as long as they paid taxes. However, the celebration of Yom Kippur was changed to Ramadan and Jewish dietary restrictions were abandoned. Eight years after fleeing Mecca for his safety, Mohammed's army returned and captured the city. The momentum of the new religion continued, combining Islam and the state, and though Mohammed died, within eighty years of his death Islam had extended from Spain to the East Indies. In his life Mohammed had ten wives and at least two concubines.

ZEALOTS IN HISTORY

⧡

One similarity exists between the stories of Jesus and Mohammed; neither could read or write, and their stories were written long after their deaths by entrepreneurs who recognized the potential power structure. Special interests are whetted by the recognition that power and wealth can be extracted by preaching fear. This monetary incentive is defended by being "called" or "divinely inspired," but a bit of reason finds many discrepancies in their alibis. For example, the stories about Moses indicate fabrication derived from a very active imagination. Most biblical historians doubt Moses could have written the Pentateuch, the five books at the beginning of the Bible that constitute the Torah, and also his own obituary, but then omit the location of his burial.

Analogous or similar stories to the biblical ones have contemporary settings. The pattern or format picks a deceased person as an idol and promotes a special interest. One quite recent example is John Birch, who was virtually sanctified in the latter part of the twentieth century by the John Birch Society. The

John Birch Society might compare to the Sadducees or Pharisees in the biblical stories. The beliefs of each of these groups or societies were ultraconservative, under the guise of patriotism, and with the desire to maintain the status quo in the belief only the ultra-right had the right answers. The organizer of the John Birch Society was John Welch, who at one time was associated with a candy manufacturer in Belmont, Massachusetts.

After World War II Welch became obsessed with what he considered the communist menace in the United States. Welch championed Senator Joseph McCarthy of Wisconsin, whose fame came from alleging that the United States was being betrayed by internal subversion. McCarthy developed his own conspiracy theories using moving targets, a technique of freely listing and changing the number of communists he alleged to be in various government agencies. McCarthy's numbers fluctuated from one speech to another. Though McCarthy smeared and ruined the lives of many people, he never proved a single one of his assertions. After damaging many people's lives, McCarthy was finally censured by the Senate while he was a member of that body. In a way, the hysteria McCarthy created was reminiscent of the Massachusetts witch trials in the early history of this country, where no proofs existed, just accusations, and in the hysteria of that time a number of people lost their lives.

John Welch stumbled onto the name of John Birch from reading U.S. Senate committee documents on WWII affairs. Welch then formed the John Birch Society in December 1958, with a dozen men he invited to a meeting in Indianapolis. The aim of the society was to alert the country to the menace of communism. Welch remained the head of the society, exercising dictatorial control that he justified as the only way to build a monolithic body. Welch published his "Black Book" in which he listed people he considered communists or dupes. The list of names included the name of President Dwight Eisenhower and General George Marshall, who after World War II served as secretary of state and later as secretary of defense. Welch stated he considered Marshall "a conscious, deliberate, and dedicated agent of the Soviet conspiracy." Of President Eisenhower, Welch wrote, "My firm belief that Dwight Eisenhower is a dedicated, conscious agent of the Communist conspiracy is based on an accumulation of detailed evidence and so palpable that it seems to me to put this conviction beyond any reasonable doubt." Welch considered the outlawing of school segregation as a socialist plot, and that the Supreme Court would merge the United States with Russia without a fight. Of course, the main tools of the John Birch Society were fear and suspicion. Some of the more naïve members of the society considered Welch a messiah. Have we heard that word before?

Who was John Birch? Prior to World War II, he was a missionary in China. When war broke out, U.S. intelligence hired Birch for his knowledge of the Chinese language. At the close of WWII Birch was in north China, and accompanied a U.S. and nationalist Chinese reconnaissance party that encountered Red Chinese troops near Hsuchow, an area held by the Chinese Communists. In the company of Lt. Tung, a Chinese nationalist, Birch sought out the Communist commander. An argument ensued, and Birch, who provoked a physical struggle, was killed. His companions were taken prisoner but later released. In accompanying the reconnaissance party Birch had been instructed to act with diplomacy. The inquiry into his death determined Birch made the Communist lieutenant lose face before his own men, defied orders of the Communist sentries, barged in, and began arguing with the Chinese commander, threatening and slugging a guard. Birch had a record of being quarrelsome and had little tolerance for those who disagreed with him.

John Welch considered Birch's death as a cold-blooded attack on the United States and Christianity, and in a book published in 1954 he listed Birch as the first casualty of WWIII. But Welch's version of the incident with the Chinese Reds does not agree with Major Krause, the commander of the base in which Birch was assigned. Welch declared Birch a martyr, though he knew nothing about Birch or his beliefs. For two decades or more the John Birch Society developed and maintained an organizational structure spread across the United States, composed of fronts in an effort to shock the American people into accepting what Welch believed was a communist threat. The society's shock troops were trained to infiltrate into every group and organization in their community to build "bedrock faith" in a new morality. The keystone was the doctrine of God, at least Welch's doctrine of God. The technique of the society's fronts was to cast suspicion and doubt and to undermine established government by claiming the U.S. government was controlled by communists. It seems the technique adopted by the Birch Society paralleled that of the communism they condemned.

John Birch Society members often kept their identity a secret as they infiltrated local city councils, boards, churches, parent-teacher associations, and Scout organizations, planting suspicion and fear of the government. Society members criticized the drive in numerous communities to fluoridate public water supplies, alleging this was a communist plot. Likewise local zoning laws and bond issues for public improvements were alleged to be the work of communists. Welch believed his mission was messianic. The society's story has similarities to some biblical characters who sought control and had vested interests. Society members selected issues or events that had the potential for differences in belief and therefore could divide public opinion. In biblical times the patriarch's stories were also concocted to fit the power structure's objectives. Judging from history, concepts designed by special-interest groups worked surprisingly well to divide and conquer.

An Overview

❧

A review of the accomplishments of religion in the last two thousand years is a history of bloody wars, slavery, famines, and plagues that decimated civilizations because of lack of knowledge about health, plus corruption and brutality within religion's own organization. Just in the twentieth century, the United States participated in six wars with no record of objections from a deity. For centuries religion's power structures have institutionalized fear to extract parishioner's wealth to adorn churches with objects of gold, art, and trappings to enhance the comfort and lifestyle of the hierarchy. Though the public has yearned for peace for thousands of years it remains as elusive as ever. Simple logic would suggest that many people would think it time to look for something more effective in obtaining peace than to rely on religion's record.

In recent years, a few rays of hope for peace have appeared among nations where education has gradually introduced logic and reason into international affairs. The effect is not complete by far, but the asinine act of destroying wealth, followed by guilt that is offset by rebuilding what war destroyed, is beginning to be recognized in some levels of government and in individual morality. Likewise, a small trace of the intent of Lincolnian logic expressed more than one hundred years ago is beginning to dawn. That logic, slightly amended to be applicable to the world society in which we live, is that a society of half poor and half rich cannot continue to exist. In adopting what is becoming our nation's endless war in search of terrorists, it is increasingly evident that we are fighting symptoms rather than causes. The causes are largely poverty and lack of education. These causes will not be addressed by a continuation of our nation's history of supporting corrupt foreign governments to satisfy some of our own internal special interests.

What changes may be required to pursue an effective course to achieve peace? The greatest detriment to peace is world poverty, and a number of measures are needed to make any real impact. To begin, world population needs to be addressed. At its present rate of growth, the meager financial and aid programs are overwhelmed by increases in population. Education immediately comes to the fore, as it is proven that as education rises, the birthrate declines. The enemy to this logical approach is religion; in many countries, including the United States, religious myths keeps much of the human race in misery and poverty, and ignorance sustains antiquated power structures. In the interest of humanity governments need to reject religion's fallacy of endorsing the animal instinct of reproduction and in its place support a policy of intelligent, responsible procreation.

To assist with a responsible policy on procreation, developed nations need coordinated policies to improve education in the developing world. The contributions to education given by developed nations to developing nations should aim at a sum equal to the defense expenditure of developed nations. This could be achieved by cutting defense budgets in half to give education the kick start that is needed. Of course, such a move would meet strong opposition from special-interest groups that benefit from the status quo. The interest in peace held by the majority needs to prevail, because it is the majority that bears the brunt of bad policy that produces debt financing and the wars caused by religious hate.

Realistically, terrorism will not be eliminated by armies and prayers; terrorism is caused by social, economic, and military policies. Turkey can be cited as an example of what can be achieved with enlightened leadership. President Kemal Ataturk of Turkey (1923–38) modernized his country with a program of funding the education for Turkish students attending foreign universities. In the United States, Secretary of State Cordell Hull, who served during the early Roosevelt administrations, assisted the Turkish government's program, making it possible for many Turkish students to attend U.S. universities. If world peace is ever to occur, abrupt changes in the priorities of developed nations will be necessary, and quite likely the quality of leadership must change as well. The latter, the quality of leadership, is the responsibility of the voting public, which today is suffers from a declining interest. Voter apathy is a result of a system that allows major funding for campaigns to come from special interests. The result is virtually a lifetime job for the conformist. Term limits are needed to obtain representation for the public, but to date the public is not concerned.

Throughout history the drag on human progress by religion and its myths is beyond the ability to calculate. The power structure of mythmakers as they used the forces of fear, murder, and suppression of education is religion's documented record. How could it happen? The human mind is easily brainwashed as is repeatedly demonstrated today. The early discoverer of scientific facts was invariably a deist, a nonbeliever. The reason?

To begin with, they were usually knowledgeable in philosophy and the humanities. Logic and reason led them beyond the closed capsule of religion, making scientific discovery possible. Today the technician, even the scientist who occasionally is documented as a believer, is far from the equal of the early scientist's understanding of the universe, of history, and of the humanities. The fully educated individual is as rare today as ever. Education systems tend to produce human robots, which unfortunately is often the safest role on the job and in society. A common contradiction is the scientific mind that requires precision and proof yet believes in a religion that is founded entirely upon hearsay and a history of violence. Fortunately, our courts have advanced beyond accepting hearsay as admissible in determining justice.

Hope remains as long as freedom of thought and expression exist. However, the continuing pursuit of militarism keeps encroaching on these essential factors for human progress.